the 7% SOLUTION

YOU *CAN* AFFORD A COMFORTABLE RETIREMENT

JOHN H. GRAVES

CLU, ChFC

SAFE HARBOR INTERNATIONAL PUBLISHING

The 7% Solution
You *Can* Afford a Comfortable Retirement
by John Graves, CLU, ChFC

Safe Harbor International Publishing
10790 Encino Drive
Oak View, CA 93022

This publication is designed to provide accurate and authoritative information in regard to the subject matter covered. It is sold with the understanding that neither the author nor the publisher is engaged in rendering legal, accounting, securities trading or other professional services. If legal advice or other expert assistance is required, the services of a competent professional person should be sought.

ISBN 978-0-9835731-2-8

FIRST EDITION
Library of Congress Cataloging-inPublication Data has been applied for.

Cover and interior design
by GKS Creative, gkscreative.com

Printed in the United States of America

TABLE OF CONTENTS

INTRODUCTION

If you are approaching retirement, it is time for you to think about your income sources. How much will you need? Where will it come from? How long will it last?

You have been told for the past three decades that you must save more, that you haven't saved enough, and that what you have saved will disappear before you do. You've been warned that the income you will receive from your meager retirement savings will be insufficient, and that inflation and health care costs will devastate your portfolio. In many cases, that simply isn't true.

Can you afford to retire? Yes, you can afford to retire comfortably if you have these habits:

+ you are a good saver
+ you are debt adverse
+ you have flexible spending habits
+ you give back to your community

Many folks in the Baby Boom generation practice these habits. There are 74 million of us, born between 1946 and 1964. Members of our cohort began to turn 65 in 2011 and will continue to do so for the next 18 years. We were taught these good habits by our parents, who learned from theirs. We live within our means, whether we use a formal budget or simply do so intuitively.

As a whole, we use debt wisely—if only because our fathers and mothers put the fear of God into us, hinting that we might be evicted and sent to debtors' prison if we missed even one payment on the house or car.

As circumstances change, we adjust our spending habits. When times are good, we take a holiday. When times are bad, we cut back and clip coupons. If we know there is a major expense coming up, we save for it.

We were taught to give back. Contributing to a church, temple, or community charity was integral to our way of life. We learned that giving a portion of our treasure—however meager—led to a sense of prosperity greater than mere money.

If saving, avoiding debt, adjusting spending, and giving back are absent from your life, you'll either get them into your life or you'll work until you drop.

Some of us have 18 more years to save for retirement; some have just a few years. It should be obvious to all that the closer we are to retirement, the more we need to have saved and the more we need to save.

You must take responsibility for your own future.

Very simple. Neither the governments of the nation nor of your state have the resources to pay you what they say they owe you. If you are less than 60, expect to wait a few more years for Social Security. If you will have a state pension, you'd better have an alternative income source, because state pensions are universally underfunded. This book isn't about politics, it's about facts. These pensions may never disappear completely, but they may very well be "adjusted" as time passes. Save for yourself. Accept responsibility for your own retirement.

This book will empower you to design
your own retirement portfolio.

Most in the financial services industry disagree that this is advisable or even possible. They argue that you need to be led to the correct decisions about your retirement. They feel that you lack the ability to make informed decisions about the markets that will fund your retirement. They strongly suggest that *their* financial wisdom is a necessary condition for your success.

Most financial planners have no idea how to do what you will learn in this book. They are simply asset gatherers who turn your hard earned savings over to a mutual fund or other financial construct. They follow a pathway set up by others, as ants do. The pheromone laid down by the ant ahead tells the follower where to go. If the pheromone leads to the nest, the ant will return home. If it leads in a circle, the ants will march around until they fall over exhausted and die. Do not use ants for your capital management!

The truly independent financial advisor has far more to offer than portfolio design and maintenance. But if portfolio design and maintenance is all you need, by hiring a financial planner you are paying a king's ransom for fool's gold. If you hire someone to watch over your capital, you are the fool. Or as Warren Buffet puts it: "If you are a half-hour into a game of cards and don't know who the patsy is, you are the patsy." Realize this verifiable fact: 2.3% of all mutual funds outperform the S&P 500 index over 1-, 5-, 10-, 15-, 20-, and 25-year rolling time frames. If you don't want to design your portfolio, then use a portfolio of low cost, no load funds or ETFs that controls your overhead and may result in at least par performance. Active management is a loser's game—except for the active managers. They make a fortune off your ignorance.

"But these people have MBAs and PhDs and CFAs!" you protest. "They have experience and knowledge. All I have is my 401(k) portfolio. How can I be as smart as the professional players in the market?"

There are three answers to this question.

First, you know your situation far better than anyone in the financial services industry knows it. This is important because:

> *Knowledge of your financial reality is the*
> *starting point for all investment decisions.*

You have been making financial decisions all your life. You are far more skilled than most advisors are willing to give you credit for. Unlike medical decisions or tax decisions or career decisions that usually require expert guidance and advice, financial decisions are best made from your perspective. Yes, you need to have a working set of "tools and rules" to manage your retirement. But these are not mysterious skills requiring the hands of a master financial engineer. You're perfectly capable of acquiring these skills.

Second, financial professionals have no skill at prediction. None of us! Repeat that each time you hear one of us make a prediction. None of the financial intelligentsia accurately predicted the market debacles of 1987, 1989, 1994, 1997, 2000, 2003, or 2008. All of our wisdom and experience didn't foresee the storms on the horizon.

Third—and perhaps most importantly—the market theories on which financial professionals rely consistently fail to perform as expected. They often fail to deliver in the best of times. Modern portfolio theory, asset allocation, diversification, and efficient frontiers significantly fail when the storm arrives. When they fail, all assets tend to fall in unison. Rather than offering an exit strategy, these theories run investors off a cliff like lemmings falling to the sea. It is unwise to follow these precepts blindly.

Strategies such as buy and hold, theories of the efficient market, and tactical tools such as mutual funds have cost you capital. They have wasted your funds. They have delayed your retirement years. They are responsible for much heartache and hand-wringing.

If you are what you eat, then your portfolio is what you invest.

These days we settle for non-nutritious, instant food in place of healthy sit-down meals. Similarly, we are far too accepting of quick-fix, prepackaged products from the financial industry. These products are stripped of healthy nutrients by processing at each step along the way. Commissions, fees, turnover, management changes, charges, biases, and taxes reduce the whole grain of individual stocks to the pap of breakfast flakes.

The 7% Solution offers real sustenance. Here you will find time-tested, down-to-earth information to guide your investment decisions as you store up your proverbial retirement harvest. Don't worry that you're not up to the task. As trader Chuck Smith says, "It ain't rocket surgery." The information available today to the least aware of us far exceeds what investment guru Benjamin Graham had at his disposal half a century ago. You can tap into this information in an ever increasingly easy manner. In most cases it is free, or nearly so. Although it's in numerical form, the information is quite easy to digest once you get the hang of it. Try putting together the tricycle for your grandson following the slightly Chinese instructions. If you can do that, you can manage your portfolio.

Yes, designing and monitoring a portfolio entails more than just putting pieces together. You'll need to spend some time at this, and you'll need to pay attention, follow your gut, and stick with your ideas. But once it's established, the portfolio will demand little effort from you. You'll even be able to automate much of this investment process.

The book is called *The 7% Solution* because it will show you how your investment portfolio may generate as much as a 7% distribution rate for your retirement income. You'll also learn:

+ How to determine your retirement income need
+ How to identify your sources of income in retirement
+ How to evaluate, select, monitor, and manage a variety of investments, from simple to more complex

The 7% Solution refutes the advice you hear from the typical investment advisor. While controversial, this is meant to be instructive rather than combative. Most investment advice is unduly influenced by the profits the advisor and fund companies reap in the form of fees. Fees kill performance: be aware.

This book is a gift to investors. It follows directly in the warm footsteps in the sand of *The Investment Answer* by Gordon Murray and Dan Goldie. The ideas expressed here are based upon three decades of experience, thousands of mistakes, and a few hundred right choices. May you benefit from that experience.

These recent times have changed our wealth in myriad ways. Perhaps you worry because you do not know what is to come. This book may alleviate much of that worry.

Yes, you will find a pathway to a comfortable retirement. You can do this!

WORKSHEET

Assignment: Write your retirement "Bucket List."

1. When do you want to retire?

2. Where do you want to retire?

3. What do you want to do when you retire?

4. How do you want to retire—in other words, what will your lifestyle be?

5. With whom do you want to retire?

Take your time thinking about these questions and write them out in as much detail as possible.

1

THE 7% SOLUTION

"The object in life is not to be on
the side of the majority, but to escape
being in the ranks of the insane."
—Marcus Aurelius

Retirement planning begins with you.

While that may seem obvious, this concept refutes much of the advice you've heard from the financial advisory community. Rather than beginning from the center—you and your current financial situation—most financial advisors typically subject you to a "strategic asset allocation" process. Erring against your best interests, they put you into the herd. They corral you. They prepare your funds for the capital chute. This way slaughter lies.

It has happened at least half a dozen times during the past thirty years. Markets collapse. Asset allocation models break down. Mutual funds lose billions. Yet most financial advisors remain in business, holding their clients' hands, waiting for recovery. After all, they still get paid. The fund companies still take their pound of flesh, collecting their 12-1b fees each year.

This book will teach you to design your own portfolio, rather than relying on a "strategic asset allocation" process. It is a challenge to all of those who feel better equipped by experience and knowledge to make financial decisions for you.

You undoubtedly have a number of questions as you contemplate your retirement, to wit:

When can I retire? How much will I need? How long can I expect my portfolio to last? How should I respond—in my portfolio and my lifestyle—during a recession? How much can I spend during the good times without undermining my retirement plan? Can I really do this on my own?

> **This book will teach you to design your own portfolio, rather than relying on a "strategic asset allocation" process.**

The 7% Solution will help you to answer these questions with confidence. But before we get into how it works, it's important to understand one of the key factors of the formula: the Baby Boomer.

Excluding the very poorest and the very wealthiest, Baby Boomers comprise 32 million households.[1] Each year from 2011 through 2029, between 3.5 million and 4.3 million of us will turn 65.[2] The public pension system known as Social Security will be heavily burdened to carry this load.[3] We are also living longer, healthier lives: life expectancy is expected to grow from 76 today to 84 over these decades.

Americans have the oldest retirement age in the developed world. Between 1998 and 2004, those who did not plan to retire at 65 rose from 36% to 57%. This reflects, among other things, improved health and the desire for personal fulfillment. In fact, the number one reason Boomers give for working longer is personal job satisfaction. As we age, we will remain active, healthy, and supportive of our children financially.[4]

Baby Boomers: Better Prepared Than They Think

Rumor has it that those of us in the Baby Boom generation will suffer a slow, taxing decline as our health deteriorates, our mind atrophies, and our wallets dry up. Supposedly, we have too little money set aside to retire. Our gut overhangs our future. The kids want their inheritance now. The environment is destroying us, as we destroy it. The future is dark, dismal, and without hope.

These rumors are greatly exaggerated.

We Boomers were raised with an attitude of adaptability. We could not see past the front door but we knew we could make it. Everyone around us could make it. Our parents trained us to work hard, pray hard, and live modestly. Many of us continue in this Pollyanna attitude of opportunity. During our retirement, we plan to remain flexible; to work or play as we choose. If we can afford "it," we may get "it." If we can't, then we will wait until we don't want "it" anymore.

Are we encumbered with an impossible dream or do we have what it takes to succeed in retirement? Each of us must answer this question in our own fashion. Is the future bright—or is it dreary? If you are of the former persuasion, then we can work together. You believe you can retire comfortably. We must work at it each year, yes, but we believe we can do it.

We are not alone in this belief. According to Joel Kotkin,[5] the Japanese word *sokojikara* implies a proven adaptability, a reserve of strength. Many of us have that reserve of strength. It was taught us by our parents, bequeathed to us by our grandparents. We can adapt. So will our portfolios. They will flex with the times, the markets, and our needs.

We emerge from a previous generation of savers and have, until 1994, followed in their footsteps: from 1945 through 1993, the average savings rate for the US population was 7%.[6] Only since the mid-nineties has it dropped—and in 2010, it returned to its previous long-term figure of 7%. We Baby Boomers save a greater amount. As we approach our retirement, most of us realize the need to build our nest for the years ahead. We save our discretionary income in retirement plans at work, in IRAs, in banks, and in insurance companies. Perhaps we own rental real estate. Perhaps we have a family business. Our assets have grown over the years through hard work and good fortune. We have contributed to them our fiscal and sweat capital. Soon, we shall turn to them for our sustenance.

We have squirreled away more than $12 trillion in equities and money markets and another $8 trillion in bank deposits. In addition, we stand to inherit another $5 trillion from our families. As a generation we have saved and will inherit a substantial sum of capital. It is not equally divided among us all; inequality is part of the game. We understand.

The habit of saving is part of the financial attitude that our parents taught us. Can you recall having an allowance as a child and being told to save some of it? Perhaps you saved for a bicycle, or a new doll. When you had a paper route, when you worked as a soda jerk or as a busgirl, your folks made you save some of your weekly income. Perhaps you had to tithe 10% too.

We also learned frugality. Whether it was sharing a bedroom with a younger sibling or wearing an older sibling's clothing, the lesson was clear: You made do and you made it last. The throwaway society came later, much later. If something broke, we watched our dad repair it, or Mr. Clarke, across the street. We also played outside, until all hours. When mom called us for dinner, we came running, no questions asked, washed our hands, sat down to our plate, folded our hands, and listened intently to the prayer of thanksgiving each night.

Mom let us lick the S&H green stamps. We were excited when we went to the stamp store; it was fun helping her decide between the floor lamp and the toaster. Mom often made our clothes, too.

Frugal savers with an eye to the Heavens: that was our training ground. While our kids may have forgotten these lessons—or perhaps never learned them—we still have them. They are translated today into these facts: Most of us—57%[7] —have no debt against our home and little or no credit card debt;[8] many of us still have mementos from high school, including textbooks; 84% of us believe in God, and more than 60% attend religious services monthly.

Our habits of frugality and saving are still intact for the most part. We have cash in the bank for emergencies or opportunities. Our home is paid off, or nearly so. The amount we have deferred into our retirement accounts has grown quietly—it may have fallen somewhat in 2008, but not as much as the market. We worry about the future; we don't think we have saved enough but believe we can do so. We also know how to live within our means. Our future opportunity is defined by our past frugality, present savings habits, and future aspirations.

Finally, we are conservative in our views toward life. Slow and steady wins the race. We have become the Joneses with whom others wished to keep up. While we may enjoy the vista from a mountain top, we are eager to get back to the clubhouse! We are gregarious, friendly, and open to sharing and listening. We have our opinions, but are not usually forceful in their expression.

These traits—frugal and savings-oriented, faithful and faith-based, flexible and fiscally conservative—define our generation.

Eighty-six percent of workers who are saving for retirement are confident in their ability to save and invest wisely.[9] We are not the lost generation—far from it. We are reasonably confident of our abilities, with our eyes to the future and our hands to the wheel.

Even if you don't identify with this image of the typical Baby Boomer, you probably have greater strength in reserve than you give yourself credit for. To make the most of your resources—both material and spiritual—read on.

The 7% Solution

The 7% Solution suggests that you can earn as much as 7% income from your portfolio. It is an alternative to the capital slaughter chute of "strategic asset allocation" and other cookie-cutter plans foisted on an unsuspecting public by sometimes lazy and unscrupulous financial advisors.

Of course, there are many in the financial profession who honestly take your best interests to heart. If you think that bothering with numbers is a fool's game and you have no interest in finance, seek out an advisor who is driven to your success. You should expect more from a good advisor than mere portfolio management. Find one who will respond to your special needs and work closely with that person. We'll discuss investment advice and individual responsibility in Chapter 3.

If, like the majority of Baby Boomers, you are a good saver, you are debt averse, and you are flexible in your spending habits, then when you retire you will have saved considerably, you will be debt free or nearly so, and you will spend according to your needs. You will also have a fair idea of what your family spends each month. That knowledge will tell you how much you need during retirement.

First, we'll take a look at your non-investment income sources. These income sources may be Social Security, a pension, rentals, or perhaps an inheritance. Next, we'll look at your investment portfolio. This is typically an IRA rollover, but it can include any capital investment.

Knowing what income you will need for a comfortable retirement allows you to design your capital to that income need. You will maintain your portfolio to give you the income necessary to supplement your non-investment income sources. Once you know your monthly expenses in retirement, then you can easily answer the question: How much do I need to earn? The answer to that question can be as much as 7%.

Let's take an easy example. You think you will need $5,000 monthly when you stop working. You know you will receive $1,500 from Social Security and your spouse will receive $1,000. You will also net $1,500 from your two rentals. You are short another $1,000 a month. You have $200,000 in your 401(k) at work that you will rollover to an IRA when you leave in April. You need to earn $1,000 monthly—or $12,000 a year—from this $200,000 in capital. You need to invest it to earn 6%. You wouldn't mind earning 7%.

How do you invest to earn that return?

In the following chapters we will review the investment vehicles that can help you attain your 7%: stocks, bonds, and more. Chapters 5 through 7—stocks, bonds, and funds—show you the simple path. Chapters 8 through 10—annuities, MLPs, BDCs, REITS, etc.—show a deeper path. If you find the complexity of investments described in Chapters 8 through 10 daunting, go directly to Chapter 11, "Designing the 7% Portfolio." A set of examples will show you how to implement the strategy using the simpler vehicles. If you choose the deeper path, more work will be required—and greater rewards may potentially be attained.

Investment Type	Rate of Return
One-year Bank CD	1 to 15%
Bonds	1 to 16%
Stock Dividends	1 to 18%
Real Estate	2 to 14%
Annuities	2 to 12%
CRTs	5 to 12%
Preferred Stocks	6 to 8%

Figure 1: Rates of Return by Investment Type, 1981 to 2010

Take a look at Figure 1 showing rates of return for a variety of investment types. As you can see, each of these investment categories offered a wide spectrum of returns between 1981 and 2011. These returns can be in the form of interest, dividends, or capital gains. You can see that bank CDs have offered from 1% interest to as much as 15% interest. Bonds have generated 1% to 16% interest. Dividends from a stock can vary from 1% to 18%. Real estate may have net income of 2% through 14%. Annuities can vary between 2% and 12%. Charitable trust income distributions can be as low as 5% or as high as 12%. Preferred stocks work within a fairly narrow range, typically 6% to 8%. International stocks and bonds can vary across the range of possible returns. Their return is a result not only of the distribution rate itself but of exchange rates—the value of the dollar versus the currency in which they are denominated.[10] We'll discuss which combination of these potential tools can help you best achieve your own 7% solution.

The Many Faces of Income

Deriving income from your capital portfolio is just one of several ways to fund your retirement. In fact, there are many ways to do so. Later in the book we'll explore alternative investment strategies such as the sale of a business, charitable gifting, and annuities. The income game is played on several fields. It's about more than just portfolio design.

If you have a deep involvement in your community—whether it is your church, synagogue, social group, or charity—you can support it in many ways. You give of your time and talent, of your energy and tools. You make gifts of material and capital. Under the right circumstances, these gifts can be very generous—to your charity and to you. The IRS guidelines should be viewed as the rules of the game. Learn to play it and win by the rules. We'll discuss tax advantages in greater detail in Chapter 13.

Many of you have worked your entire lives in your own business. You have nurtured it from the kitchen table to the manufacturing floor, from the typewriter to the computer. You may have a service, a product, or a combination of both. When it comes time to retire, you will either want out—or you'll be dragged out upon your last breath! If you want out, you have to find a market for the company: you have to sell it. The process of identifying the market, finding buyers, agreeing upon a fair price, and being properly paid takes more than a little time. It is worth the effort. We'll discuss how taking the proceeds from the sale of a business can impact your retirement.

Annuities are among the oldest of capital holding devices. Ancient Rome employed them. Medieval Europe and Renaissance England enriched the concept, sharpened the tool. Social Security is an annuity. We all have them and use them. Yet because they are as common as thread, we ignore how they bind us in the woof and warp of capital. We'll review how private annuities issued by insurance carriers can contribute to your retirement.

The amount of wealth that will pass from our parent's generation to us over the next 20 years is enormous: $5 trillion. That number is estimated to grow to $25 trillion by the year 2050.[11] Seven percent of us will receive 50% of this wealth. The median inheritance is estimated at less than $50,000. The top 5% will receive more than $237,000.[12]

Yes, some will inherit much. Few will so inherit, however. For those who will receive the accumulated capital from their parents' hard work and diligent saving, the effects can be both promising and devastating. It is a once-in-a-lifetime event and difficult to prepare for. The amount will vary for each of you. What will you decide to do with it? We'll discuss the impact of inheritance on your retirement planning.

Sources of income during retirement are as varied as your background, as simple as your needs. You will be able to use many of these ideas. You can skip over those that do not apply.

How you design and maintain your portfolio will be integral to its success. We'll coach you on how to pick the individual pieces and show you how they fit together into the complex whole. We'll discuss what investments to hold, what to monitor, and when to walk away. The book will teach you always to view your retirement portfolio as an organic reflection of your needs—not the market's.

> We will mature, retire, and move through our end-game with grace.

We Baby Boomers will retire. We will do so in our own manner, each according to his or her principles and abilities. Some will enjoy the RV; some the second home. Some will work; many will play. Some will struggle more than others.

WORKSHEET

Assignment: Summarize your retirement income sources: estimate the amounts for each item below to determine your approximate total income per month.

1. Will you receive a pension? How much per month?

2. Will you receive Social Security? How much per month?

3. Do you have an IRA? How much income will it generate per month?

4. Do you have a 401(k)? How much income will it generate per month?

5. Do you have stocks? How much income will they generate per month?

6. Do you have bonds? How much income will they generate per month?

7. Do you have mutual funds? How much income will they generate per month?

8. Do you have cash accounts? How much income will they generate per month?

9. Do you have other investments? How much income will they generate per month?

10. Will you work? How much income will you generate per month?

2

BRINGING YOUR RETIREMENT INTO FOCUS

Plus ca change, le plus c'est la même chose.
The more things change, the more they stay the same.
Changement est normal.
Change is normal.

Financial planning and investing are usually presented to the public in a static, one-size-fits-all fashion. As Henry Ford said, "You can have any color car you want—as long as it is black."
The typical financial plan available for public consumption, whether online or from a financial advisor, assumes certain facts. These facts—your expenses, inflation, an asset allocation format—are then assumed to continue in a straight line throughout your retirement years. In fact, nothing will be static through your retirement years. The only thing that doesn't change is change.

You Are Unique—Your Retirement Plan Should Be, Too

An investment process should reflect your current financial situation, which will change as time passes. Your portfolio should change to reflect *your* needs first, the market second. Yet a significant majority of financial advisors, registered representatives, and stockbrokers will suggest a portfolio that bears an extraordinary resemblance to your neighbor's portfolio. You may have a bit more small cap and emerging market than she. She may have more high-yield bond funds than you. The difference is one of style and technique, rarely one of substance over form.

This constancy of advice perpetuates many financial myths. The first is the myth of correlation: Assets that have low correlation—that are unlike one another—allow for better performance. Another myth: Different eggs in different baskets; diversification leads to lower volatility. Better to listen to Mark Twain's advice: "Put all your eggs in one basket—and watch that basket very carefully!"

Here are some more examples of generic advice:

+ Invest 60% in stocks and 40% in bonds
+ Your age = the % of your portfolio you should have in bonds
+ The efficient frontier designs the mix for your portfolio
+ Buy and hold
+ Diversification is the secret to portfolio management
+ Markets are efficient tools of price discovery: listen to them

There are hundreds of these aphorisms. They are at best platitudes; at worst they are recipes for disaster. Follow any at your peril. Generic advice can be good, bad, or indifferent advice for you; it all depends on your situation. Examine the underlying assumptions before accepting them as truth. Remember that "rules of thumb" are often "rules of dumb."

Planning for your retirement must be personal. The planning must be unique to your circumstances: your experience, drives, interests, lifestyle, family, desires, prejudices, assets, expertise, community, health, income, tax brackets, life expectancy, and any other factors only you can name. In Chapter 11 we'll explain how you can bring all these factors together to tailor a portfolio to your needs—not your neighbor's or financial advisor's.

A Few Revolutionary Ideas

Let's get a few ideas out into the open immediately. Warning: these ideas run counter to most generally agreed upon principles of financial planning and portfolio management.

1. When you retire, you will need less capital than you have been told you need.
2. Your annual income needs will fluctuate with your personal situation, with the economy, with your age, and with your health.
3. You may live longer than you think.
4. Financial models used to design portfolios are cartoons. Follow them at your peril.
5. The key assumption of most retirement planning tools—a 4% rate of return—is too low a target. It almost certainly assures failure.
6. Simple approaches to retirement issues are fine *if* they are also flexible.
7. Portfolio challenges that you face as an individual are different from those a portfolio manager faces.
8. You need to listen to your head, your heart, and your stomach during retirement, in no particular order. Each will have its time to prevail and its time of silence.

These eight ideas are presented to you, the investor, as opportunities. They will empower you to enjoy a comfortable retirement, one free from the rigorous application of silly rules that have no relationship to the real world of your personal retirement. They are presented as challenges to the investment community. A gauntlet has been thrown down to the trusted financial advisor who puts everyone into the same grab bag of asset allocated mutual funds, who tells clients to invest for the long run, and who believes in the efficient market hypothesis.

Where will your income during retirement come from? There are myriad choices: Social Security; public or private pensions; work—of choice or necessity; rental property; hobbies turned into businesses; consulting services turned into enterprises; charitable trusts; inheritances; perhaps even a lottery win or a good day in Vegas. You can name many other income sources.

Note that we have not yet included the investment portfolio. That is another choice; a choice taken once all other income sources are considered. At the very least it's a choice taken in conjunction with all others.

Once all sources of income are considered and these amounts are compared to your annual projected (guesstimated!) need, portfolio income can be addressed. For example, if you need an additional $12,000 a year after all your other income sources are added up, you would divide that amount by the size of your investment portfolio—let's say it's $172,000—to find your required rate of return. As long as that rate is reasonable—7% or less—you can structure your portfolio to generate the required amount each month, directly deposited into the your bank account.

As a retiree, your investment portfolio is first and foremost an income portfolio.

As a retiree, your investment portfolio is first and foremost an income portfolio. Growth is no longer the most important aspect of it. Growth is secondary to income. Repeat this each morning as you look in the mirror—ten times. Income takes precedence over growth.

How do you design a portfolio for income? You do not need to use mutual funds, non-traded REITs, most annuities, or any leveraged or complex—and costly—financial products. You use institutional quality bonds, stocks with sustainable dividends, preferreds, perhaps some sovereign debt, maybe some lower quality debt. You are strict about stop losses. You can address the concern of inflation with ETFs, shortening debt maturities, and bank CDs. If this sounds too complex, take heart—each investment vehicle will be explained in the coming chapters.

Investing in Value Rather Than the Theory du Jour

Benjamin Graham has been a master of the marketplace since the 1920s. You may not have heard of him. You probably haven't read him. You should consider reading him as you read this book.[1] For that matter, once you read him, you may realize that you don't need to read anything else. After all, Warren Buffet, Charlie Munger, David Dodd, and a few dozen other very successful investors have followed his ideas for some time with a modicum of success.

Graham's ideas are simple: buy stocks of companies whose price is less than their current value. Own individual bonds of companies that have the ability to pay their debts. Look for firms that can afford their dividend and have made this distribution for many years. Buy bonds with significant coverage ratios. Use moderation in portfolio design. Be prepared for failure!

Value investing suggests that playing a hand well is more important than playing a winning hand—if you do so, you will eventually win the game.

The knowledgeable investor has the time and the inclination to design, implement, and maintain a portfolio. The process hasn't changed significantly over the previous 75 years. It is rarely about math; nearly always about arithmetic.[2] It is about straightforward security analysis. You do not need to be a CFA to do this work—if anything, the depth of knowledge carried in this prestigious title can put one off the value path. A little knowledge is a dangerous thing; a lot of knowledge can paralyze you!

The ideas in *The 7% Solution* are based upon the value tenants of Graham, Buffet, Dodd, and Munger. Value ideas are not predictive. Predictions of stock prices or markets are foreign to the value concept. No one has any idea where the markets are headed or how the US or global economies will perform during the next five years or 50 years.

Other theories take different approaches: growth, modern portfolio theory, asset allocation, buy and hold, efficient markets. There are dozens of approaches. Many of these have a predictive assumption designed into them. Their assumption is: markets are for the most part reasonable, rational, and can be analyzed with some precision. Taking risk is rewarded long term with higher returns.

This assumption—the rational market—too often proves false. When it does, you lose. As we said earlier, market theories consistently fail to perform as expected. Non-rational behavior has occurred with significant regularity in the markets. As Keynes has said, "The markets can stay irrational longer than I can stay solvent."

The value approach aspires to adequate performance. Adequate performance meets your individual retirement income need. It is adequate to your situation. This is not mediocrity. It is not passive. Value investing assumes you:

+ Are capable of learning about a company and its market;
+ Are willing to establish defenses around your portfolio;
+ Wish to play well, rather than to "beat the market."

Transacting with Mr. Market

Benjamin Graham used the metaphor of Mr. Market early in his writing career.[3] It is a simple tool to understand markets. Mr. Market will appear at your door each day to offer you a price at which you may acquire or dispose of securities. If you ignore him, he will return tomorrow with a new offer to buy or sell. He does not care what you do. He will not be affronted by your behavior. You should not be slighted by his.

He may be rational for months at a time, then a raving loony for a week or so. He may become "normal" again—whatever that means—or he may act in a "new normal" fashion. Over the years, you will be amazed at his range of performances. He is a cross between Tom Waits and Alan Greenspan!

Rational behavior is just one of a number of behavioral choices that Mr. Market can make. He can be emotional, psychic, psychotic, irrational, or fulsome with enterprise. He can also be just plain wrong. He can be the superlative example of Rational Man or a ranting maniac. He can be controlled by crony capitalists, governmental regulations, or events entirely outside of his venue. He can ignore all controls.

You cannot predict his behavior. No one can. Run from those who say they know how to predict his behavior. They are far more dangerous to your success than he is. Predictive skill is a contradiction in terms. In ancient Rome, a college was established and run for a thousand years to teach the reading of entrails. Today we call it technical analysis.

Predictions are based upon knowledge of secret meanings, illumined only to the cognoscenti. For a small fee they may tell your fortune. You may choose to believe in these things, but they have no basis in the reality of the markets. They are belief systems, faith based, complete with saints and sinners, sacraments and tithes.

Human behavior—and that of Mr. Market—does not have to have a predictive component to it.

As a value investor, you are patient. You have no need to jump when Mr. Market appears at your door. You understand that he will be at your door every trading day with prices for you. He is your source of information. He works for you. He is not your master. You are not a slave to his information. If he is reasonable, he will work with you in a rational manner to achieve your income goal. He is quite often a rational guy.

When he is irrational—more often than many are willing to admit—you have two choices. Choice one: ignore him. Do not answer the door. Often this is the best approach. He will quiet down eventually. You do not have to transact with Mr. Market. When he goes into his paroxysm of rage and madness, simply close the door. Choice two: tell him you have no need for his information. If you have no securities positions (because you are not invested in the stock markets), he can only offer you new prices on other stocks. You don't have to accept. When you don't accept, you have made the decision that the risks in the marketplace outweigh the potential rewards. You are on a "risk holiday." No decision to make. When Mr. Market calms down, you will consider his offers again.

As a value investor, you have two portfolios: your current team (your investments) and the stable (of alternative stocks). You always have other choices. You realize you make mistakes and Mr. Market often misprices. When either of these occurs, you sell—your stop loss will trigger you when to do this. The proceeds go to your money market account. Now you can choose your next position from the stable. You are ready to run the next race.

Most important, as a value investor, your portfolio is self-generated. It is a result of your actions and objectives. Each of you will have a slightly different point of view, which will be reflected in your portfolios.

Now That I Don't Take Generic Advice, How Do I Invest?

Rather than predictions, look for important information, such as low debt to equity and a strong history of dividend payments to shareholders. Understand how that information may be of value to your portfolio. Analyze it with respect to your retirement income need. In subsequent chapters you'll discover many ways to do this.

Each approach to portfolio analysis has its limitations and opportunities. Expect these. Do not expect a panacea, a magic potion. Value investing, growth at a reasonable price, buy and hold, charting, timing—all are simply examples of our rational understanding of a non-rational beast: Mr. Market. Sometimes they work, sometimes they don't.

Mr. Market is neither a fool nor a wise man. He comes to your door each day to offer you a price at which he may buy from you or sell to you. He is agnostic. You too are agnostic. He is there for only one reason—to provide you with information. You must determine the validity and usefulness of that information, according to your financial situation. You may ignore him or accept his offer. You are always flexible. You never allow him to dictate to you. You can never blame him for your decisions.

Your income needs will drive your discussions with Mr. Market. *All else is secondary to decisions about your personal financial situation.* For example, if you need to earn a minimum of 6% and Mr. Market is presenting you with 5%, you know that you will not want to transact with Mr. Market on that investment.

How will you support the family during retirement? Only you know that. Only you can solve that problem. It is a problem that will change as you voyage through retirement. Remember: *Changement est normal*—change is normal. Your response to Mr. Market will change as your needs change. He will provide you with information. You will use that information to achieve personal financial freedom.

WORKSHEET

Assignments:

1. Read the Introduction, pages xiv–xv, and pages 131-144 of *The Intelligent Investor* by Benjamin Graham.

2. Read pages 83-84, "The Lesson of Mr. Market," in *Benjamin Graham on Investing* by Janet Lowe.

3

FIRST THINGS FIRST: CAPTURING YOUR DATA

> "Begin at the beginning and go on
> till you come to the end; then stop."
> **—Lewis Carroll**

ou are the captain on your voyage to retirement. But before embarking on the building of your retirement portfolio, you must first gather all the data you can about your current and future income and expenses.

First: Gather Your Expense Data

Let's begin with your current living expenses. You can start with data from memory, from your checkbook, or from a combination of both. The entries can be factual or interpretive. The facts may be records of each year's costs. Or the facts can be anecdotal, illustrating only this year's or this week's expenses. A few keep very accurate records; the remainder work at it. This is not a criticism; it is simply an observation from 26 years of data gathering. If we can get within 25% of your actual living expenses, we are doing a fair job of approximating your financial daily jog.

This data is then viewed mathematically. There are many retirement planning software packages on the market. A Monte Carlo run—which simulates a few sources of uncertainty and determines average values over a range of outcomes—is often used today. More complex models allow for a variety of data changing inputs: inflation, changes in expenses over time, life expectancies, income sources, and inheritances, to name a few. The resulting information may be viewed graphically, numerically, or both. Changes may be made in real time or in future time.

The results are interpreted according to your current situation. Will you save more or less? Invest more conservatively or aggressively? Live a longer and healthier life? None of the answers to these questions is currently known. Answers to these questions will change the interpretation of the data. It's important to remember not to be a slave to data. You are the master here.

You'll want to use a model for your retirement income and expense projections that has enough flexibility to reflect changes in your lifestyle. You'll also want to be aware of how you spend your income, just as you'll want to be aware of how your income sources match your needs. You'll need to review the model on a regular basis, just as you review your health screening.

Remember that a model is just that and nothing more. It is an estimate of the results. It is based on a small data sampling, subject to interpretation and changeable in nearly infinite ways. Do you recall making models as a young boy or playing with dolls as a young girl? Those were models. They were not real ships, cars, or girls. Barbie is a model, she is not real! The car is fun to build, just don't try to drive it! Remember that your financial model is a representation of your money; it's not your actual money. You can't bank on it.

How can you afford to retire? Can you afford a lifetime of retirement? The solutions to these questions are a complex of results. These results depend on the assumptions, the starting points. They depend on how these assumptions are viewed mathematically—in other words, which models are run. These results are also a function of the one interpreting them: you, or an advisor, or a computer. Just because we are working with the firmness of numbers does not mean that the answers we get are firm. Models are approximations, in the vernacular of the financial professional. They are guesses. They are more Monets than Ansel Adamses.

To create a retirement financial plan, you need to answer the following questions, assigning values whenever possible.

1.   When will you retire?
2.   What are your non-work-related income sources at retirement?
3.   How are you managing these assets?
4.   What is the rate of return you expect on your assets?
5.   Will you work during retirement?
6.   What are the sources of your retirement work income?
7.   How will the economy change your lifestyle?
8.   What will you do during retirement?
9.   How long will you live?
10. How will your health affect your retirement?

The first six questions and their answers are reasonably quantifiable. The last four questions and their answers are far more subjective. Their answers are mostly guesses, dependent upon many unknown future events. The values you give to these questions will determine your complex of answers. The range of possibilities depends upon your views of the future.

You can have some control over the answers to these queries. While luck, the passage of time, circumstances, and fate will have their impact, you can still steer the ship. Remember, you are the captain of your future; you just don't know precisely where you are going or how you will get there.

Do you love or hate your career? Do you relish the thought of endless vacations to see the grandkids, or do you fear the last day on the job? You may be retired by circumstance, regulatory dictate, or company policy.

You may never retire. Your love of career and its challenges may be so integral to your life that not working is simply not a consideration. (The author would fit into this group!)

You may find yourself working part time. You may do so because you want to keep your hand in the game. The skills you have developed over a lifetime of employment are not easily relinquished for some. The drive to do well, the urge to manage, invent, direct, or assemble—all of these are to be respected.

You may find that you need to work to meet your income needs. The most logical choice would be to work in your chosen field. Consulting is a growing industry; the "elders of the community" have the most experience.

What does retirement mean to you? It usually takes six months to a year to make the adjustment to the retirement lifestyle. Your entire life will change, as it did when you got married, had children, and ultimately saw them leave home for good. You will find ways to fill the eight to twelve hours a day you used to spend working. How you fill this time will consume you for the rest of your life. The new beginning will be intimidating at first, but you will surprise yourself and your associates by how quickly you adapt.

Second: Gather Your Income Data

Once you have a clear picture of your expense situation, it's time to look at your income sources. Think of retirement income as a series of faucets. Just as in your home you have a variety of water sources, so too will you have a variety of income sources during retirement. Social Security may become the sink line, your pension the mainline, with dividend income as the drip irrigation and part-time work as the garden hose. You will open these faucets as you need them and control them to meet your income expectations. Some you can delay, some you must draw from at a certain age.

What are your income sources at retirement? The answers here can be very specific. You may have your savings and your retirement plan assets. You may have an art collection, a rental property, an inheritance, your life insurance, a portfolio of stocks and bonds, a business, your charitable contributions, the family partnership. Answers can be as simple or as esoteric as you are. You have your career skills, your experience, your knowledge, and your contacts. Your contact list may be as helpful as your IRA! The inventory you take of these income resources may be quite extensive.

Will these resources allow financial independence? The National Bureau of Economic Research in 2004 found that "holdings of elderly households suggest there is a limited decline in financial assets as households age." Most families do not spend as much as they can during their retirement. In fact, they continue to accumulate! Please keep this observation in mind when you or your spouse starts to fret about affording to retire. The fear is not based upon observable fact. Affordability is in the actions of the retiree, rather than the complaints of the media. Most Boomers have saved all of their lives for this time. Most are well prepared.

What will you work at during your retirement? Many of us take deep pleasure in our work. Having been employed for forty or fifty years, for eight or more hours a day, we view work as a big part of our lives. When we retire, we have to replace these hours with a new, rewarding pastime. If we look forward to this, then we will enjoy our new adventure.

Perhaps you will take up art as a hobby. The learning process is never ending. The friends you will make may become lifelong artistic partners. You may follow a teacher, or instructor, or artist for many years for guidance. The time may come when you want to offer your work to the community. Now you are a business person as well as an artist. The market may discover the economic value of your work. Your response will evolve within your work. The cycle will become a series of epicycles. The hobby has taken on a life of its own. The same cycle may apply to your work in the community, with the family, or elsewhere.

If we will have remorse at the loss of our career, then we will face a real challenge. The psychological effect, the emotional trauma, will be hurdles. The career change from work to retirement may be a difficult one.

What if we feel we must work during our retirement? Many will have saved insufficiently for a comfortable retirement lifestyle. We might extend our working life by a few years and delay the fearful event. Others may have to work part time to keep up with their expenses. The work may be consulting or greeting, but it will supplement our income for a few years. If you must work, then save as you work. The time will come when you will not be able to find a position. You must prepare for this time.

Third: Factor in Variations to Your Income and Expenses

Variations to your income or expenses might include any, all, or none of the following:

+ Mortgage paid off at what age?
+ Travel begins; increases; slows down; stops
+ Health improves; declines
+ Spouse dies
+ New spouse
+ Substantial change in work: increase or decrease
+ Inflation, deflation or both
+ Living expenses increase and decrease
+ Community participation (church, charity, etc.)
+ Grandchildren or children come to live with you
+ The aging process reduces your need for income

It is inappropriate to project a constant increase in income needs as time passes based solely upon an inflation factor. This is what virtually all retirement planning software has embedded in its programming. This simplistic answer to a complex question is the basis for far too many retirement planning decisions. It is simply facile! We cannot project with any degree of confidence your income needs more than a few years into the future. Even that projection is fraught with peril. Each of the above could so distort your situation that any projection is a guess. Better, at least, to project a range of possibilities that grows over time—a cone of probabilities. Each year will tell you what your retirement income needs truly are.

In reality, your retirement planning should be revisited at least every two years, to review not just your portfolio return—which is the reason for most reviews—but your lifestyle changes and how each affects the other. Portfolio and lifestyle are intertwined, each codependent, neither dominant. If your financial advisor gets this, you have a winner. If you are doing this on your own, you need to be responsive to changes in each realm.

Planning for retirement begins with fairly objective information. Note the adjective "fairly," please. You can identify your current expenses. You can do so to the degree that you have been aware of them in the past. Your check register can be a guide, as can your tax return.

Some expenses are fairly constant, like the mortgage or insurance or property taxes. Some change over time: food, repairs, subscriptions, taxes, vacations. Some are infrequent: gifts, weddings, births. Many change each year: utilities, fuel for the house and the cars, medical costs. The initial process is to identify your current cost of living.

Last But Not Least: Improve Your Numbers

Wise wealth management can allow for a substantial income difference during retirement. The ideas suggested here offer you the opportunity to review your choices during your pre-retirement years and act smartly. What are you doing to increase your assets?

The repetition may be boring, but everyone needs to know this: regular savings into the retirement plan—whether an IRA, SEP, 401(k), Roth, etc.—can be the single most important behavior you can adopt to ensure a more comfortable retirement. Do it!

Wise wealth management can allow for a substantial income difference during retirement.

Saving $5,000 each year into a retirement account earning 7% will result in $338,720 over 25 years. That amount can allow a monthly income of nearly $2,000. Start two years earlier and the savings can result in an additional $100,000, a further $580 in monthly income. Did we mention the $45,000 in taxes not paid during this time? Your money, your choice. If your employer matches, it's more for you. These taxes not paid—and thus kept in your pocket—and any matches by your employer are free raises each year that you give yourself. A few popular financial commentators disagree. You are free to ignore advice that is contrary to experience!

Another dramatic way to improve your pre-retirement assets is to reduce your debt during your working years. Eliminating the mortgage on your home is the second most valuable behavior you can adopt in anticipation of retirement. Paying off a $250,000 mortgage at 7% will reduce your expenses by $1,663 a month. You will not have to make that payment during retirement. You will have increased your monthly income by $1,663. You will own the house free and clear. Most importantly, you will be free of worry about debt!

Do you have credit card debt? Pay it off. A $25,000 balance at 18% costs you $634 a month. Want to increase your income? Pay off the cards. If you receive a bonus, use it to pay down your short-term debt. If you get a windfall—anything from an inheritance to a good lottery day to stock options—pay down the debt. Then use the $634 to take yourself and your spouse out to dinner, some place that requires a weekend stay. Get away and congratulate yourselves, reward yourselves—and pay for the trip in full when you get the bill! At that dinner commit to a new behavior: never charge what you cannot pay off each month when the bill arrives.

WORKSHEET

Assignment: Define your retirement expenses. Use the following table as a guide.

Mortgage	
Real estate taxes	
Real estate insurance	
Utilities: • electricity • gas • water • phone • TV/cable/satellite • trash	
Groundskeeper	
Food	
Entertainment	
Laundry/dry cleaning	
Personal care	
Subscriptions	
Travel	

Insurance:
• life
• business
• health
  - health club membership
  - supplements
  - prescriptions
  - copays/deductibles	

Pet care	
Child/grandchild care	
Gifts	
Taxes (typically quarterly payments)	
Tithing	
Savings	
Discretionary spending	

4

A BRIEF WORD ON INVESTMENT ADVICE

"It takes nearly as much ability to know how to profit by good advice as to know how to act for one's self."
—**Francois de la Rochefoucauld**

The purpose of this book is to empower you to wean yourself away from advisors, who are, unfortunately, often nothing more than salespeople for lucrative, prepackaged financial products. Nonetheless, if navigating your own retirement simply sounds too daunting, take heart: professional help is available. Finding good professional help will require effort on your part. A vast range of competency and honesty exists within the financial services industry, so it's imperative to get referrals, ask questions, and check references.

Before investing in a professional, it would be wise for you to have clear answers to the following questions:

- What does a financial advisor actually do?
- When it comes to your retirement, what are your financial advisor's responsibilities?
- When it comes to your retirement, what are your responsibilities?

This chapter will explore each of these important inquiries. Whether you decide to go it alone or hire a financial advisor, the hope is that you will emerge from this discussion with greater clarity about the next appropriate step for you.

What a Financial Advisor Actually Does

Many financial advisors are actually arithmetic engineers. They put pieces together for you. They are always the same pieces; they just appear in different combinations.

Financial advisors base their work on the academic writings of economists—more recently econometricians—whom they have been taught to believe. Yet these very economists and econometricians—starting with the father of the efficient market hypothesis, Eugene Fama—have essentially disavowed themselves of many previous principles that were first written up in the 1960s and 1970s. These principles have evolved, as has Dr. Fama.

The financial services industry, however, has not kept up. In fact, it is like a broken record, stuck on the same reprise: Buy and hold. Efficient markets. Efficient frontier. Asset allocation. Diversification reduces risk. These ideas have to work—don't they?

Many financial writers have essentially ignored the real world since the early 1970s. Many financial services professionals continue to march like lemmings to the sea. Markets crash. They get up and march again—and the markets crash again. Media love financial writers because they always have something to complain about, such as why the markets don't follow their well-worn rules. Unfortunately, these rules apply only in the imaginary world of Rational Man. Time and time again the financial writers are wrong. But still, they get paid—and the pay is good.

Financial planning and portfolio design are far more art than science.

Despite what you may have been led to believe by the rule makers, financial planning and portfolio design are far more art than science. Perhaps the following story will give you a better understanding of what a financial planner actually does.

Your author has a work of art on a wall in the office. It is an 18-foot-long scroll, handmade of rice paper. The ink was ground slowly, by hand, from a hard ink stick. The artwork is a portrait of a number series called the Fibonacci series. Fibonacci lived in North Africa and in Pisa in the thirteenth century. He is credited with introducing Arabic numerals to Europe, including the zero. They replaced Roman numerals. Their efficiency slowly satisfied the medieval world, which took them up over the next century. Fibonacci is directly responsible for the basic tools we use today: numbers in the decimal series and the zero.

Fibonacci also demonstrated a simple problem in arithmetic with rabbits. How many pairs of rabbits will you have after one year if, starting with one pair, they breed a new pair each month? The answer takes the digit 1, adds it to the digit 2 to arrive at the digit 3, then repeats the process: 2 added to 3 = 5, 5 + 3 = 8, 8+5 = 13, etc. (The answer, if you haven't done it yet, is 377.)

The series runs across the rice paper, each line about eight inches long with about 100 lines to the meter. The scroll is about six meters long. My client, a well-known artist, did the arithmetic with an abacus. My wife and I encountered this piece at an art exhibit and liked it immediately; she for the art work, I for the mathematical precision. We acquired it and had it framed for protection and illumination.

New clients often see the work and ask about it. I ask them to figure out the math. (Their kids always do; the adults, less often!) I explain the story behind its creation; the creator's diligent arithmetic, art, and ultimate design. Clients look at it in wonder, with new eyes. I then explain that it represents what we do as financial advisors. There is a tremendous amount of detail work in numbers. There is far more work in the artistry and design of portfolios.

The artistry is a result of experience, of the passage of time, of countless errors in judgment, of listening more than telling, of thinking, of feeling, of deeply felt passions and coldly understood equations. No amount of book learning can teach it, yet it is worthless without an extraordinary amount of reading. When the results are poor, the artistry has failed; when results are good, it glows with success.

What Are a Financial Advisor's Responsibilities?

If you have a professional financial advisor, the advisory fee may be 1% each year. This is much higher than you might incur on your own, certainly. Suppose you have a $250,000 portfolio and you've just hired a financial advisor. Her annual fee will be $2,500. What should you expect for this fee? The following is a partial list of what you might be paying for:

- Experience
- Access to information, e.g., subscription-based knowledge
- No or low transaction charges
- Financial planning software and application
- Financial advice on myriad issues
- A shoulder: someone who listens
- A foot: someone who can take action
- A head: someone who knows what they know
- A heart: someone who cares what you feel

A financial advisor should be someone you can trust, but the financial services industry attracts its fair share of unscrupulous practitioners. Keep in mind what P. T. Barnum said in the 1840s: "There is a fool born every minute." Your financial advisor is responsible not only for working with you openly and honestly, but also for helping you to avoid fraudulent schemes in the market. You, however, share that responsibility.

What Are Your Responsibilities?

A financial advisor cannot simply review the pile of financial statements you bring to her office and come up with the perfect retirement plan for you. As we've discussed, your retirement is unique to your circumstances and will require input from you. Even if you place your retirement entirely into the hands of a financial advisor, certain responsibilities will always lie with you, such as the gathering and monitoring of expense and income data.

Choosing a Financial Advisor

If you hire a financial advisor, your reliance upon his or her expertise in designing and maintaining your retirement portfolio will be critical to your successful retirement. You (and perhaps your spouse) have brought you to this threshold. Your advisor must carry you across; must support you in this new adventure.

Your financial advisor should be willing to listen to your narrative, analyze your financial position, and design a series of solutions appropriate to your circumstances. Financial advisors should be adaptable. They should avoid having agendas. At the very least, they must be able to follow your guidelines and help you to maintain your retirement lifestyle. They should be able to do the work you prefer to proffer to them. If they try to fit you into an investment style, technique, model, or portfolio of their choosing, you may want to continue your search.

How do you find a good financial advisor? Referrals are always best. If you have friends who appear to have peace of mind as well as wealth, ask them if an excellent financial advisor is the key to their serenity—and get the number! You might ask your attorney or accountant for a referral. Always bring up the subject of integrity when listing your criteria for an advisor. Credentials are fine. Seek character.

If you're a reader with a penchant for numbers and a willingness to do the initial work required, you may choose to go it alone. The following chapters on stocks, bonds, and other investment vehicles will contain sufficient information to start you along this path. But whether you lean on a professional or shoulder the work alone, it is your responsibility to be informed about these investment options, as well as about taxes and other circumstances that can affect your retirement.

As the best advisors know, retirement planning is more art than science. So get out your pallet and paints—and prepare to create your future!

WORKSHEET

Assignment: Examine your portfolio performance.

1.   Ask your current advisor to create a performance report of your accounts.

2.   Review the original retirement plan you did with your advisor. Update it. Projections (guesses) of expenses are more realistic now.

3.   Ask your advisor to grade your portfolio's performance. Does she compare your portfolio to the market or to your retirement goal? Make sure the comparison takes your retirement goal into account.

STEPPING INTO STOCKS

"Business has a noble purpose. Making money is one of the important things that business does for society."
— John Mackey, CEO of Whole Foods

From at least the time of the Dutch East India Company in the 1600s—and undoubtedly even earlier—business people have raised money by selling the ownership of pieces of their companies, commonly known as shares. A share of stock is a share in the value of the corporation. When you buy the common stock of a corporation, you are participating in the ownership of that company. This entitles you to a share of its profits and its losses.

Rather than act as a primer on how stocks work, this chapter is intended to encourage you to think outside the mutual fund and to consider investigating and investing in your own stocks. Individual stocks should be an essential portion of any value investor's portfolio.

It's currently fashionable to discourage investors from purchasing stocks individually. Much of the financial advisory community contends that the ordinary investor has neither adequate knowledge about individual companies nor the resources to make informed decisions. They suggest that only institutional investors have the resources and experience to buy and sell stocks profitably. They further argue that there is too much risk in owning individual stocks, since by owning a relatively small number of stocks, the poor performance of one company can significantly affect your entire portfolio.

These arguments are grossly overstated and at the same time neglect the advantages of an individually managed investment portfolio: greater upside potential, lower potential volatility, and the peace of mind of knowing exactly what you own and how it's performing. The same diversification that is supposed to protect managed portfolios can significantly undermine their performance, as we saw in the most recent recession. In fact, real billions are made by institutional investors who move significant capital into concentrated positions, then move out upon pre-determined decision points.

The Search for Sustainable Dividends

We are going to revisit some respected, time-valued approaches and renew old acquaintances. In the case of stocks, this means dividends. Dividends are simply net profits returned to the shareholders. We hold shares. We share this risk. Shouldn't we also share directly in the profits?

As a company makes a net profit—and continues to do so year after year—it has several choices. It can:

+ Pay down debt
+ Make acquisitions
+ Reinvest in corporate capital projects

+ Repurchase stock
+ Add to the compensation structure of any, or some, employees
+ Pay a dividend

As investors, our goal in saving for and living off of our portfolios during retirement is to search out those firms that pay reasonable dividends. We are looking for stocks issued by well-run companies that have paid sustainable dividends for several years. We believe that the payment of dividends is an act of faith by the board of directors and by senior management—a faith that what they are doing will continue to reap further net profits. Dividends are a direct reflection of net profits and good growth. Dividends signal the company's confidence in the future growth of earnings.

In 1940 Graham and Dodd said, "A dollar of earnings is worth more to the stockholder if paid to him in dividends than when carried to surplus. The common-stock investor should ordinarily require both an adequate earning power and an adequate dividend." The evidence for this simple insight was best demonstrated by Dr. Jeremy Siegel in *Stocks for the Long Run.*[1]

In fact, the most recent research indicates that more than 90% of the total return for the US stock market is the result of dividends, paid and reinvested. Consider that statement for a moment. Nearly all of the total return of the stock market is from dividends.[3]

In addition to receiving the dividend yearned for by Graham and Dodd, the value portfolio actually grows better and has less volatility than the S&P 500 Index itself. The dividend-oriented portfolio outperforms not only the eponymous index, but exceeds the expectations of the efficient markets model. The highly respected financial soothsayer Gary Shilling has recently agreed, and seven out of ten Wall Street analysts surveyed by Barron's in 2010 believed that dividend paying stocks with low debt and good free cash flow were the investment of choice for today's economic and market conditions.[4]

Dividend Yield	Annualized Return*
Top quintile	13.98%
Next	12.01%
Mid	9.77%
Lower	8.59%
Lowest	9.57%
S&P 500	9.57%

*Assumes reinvestment of all dividends, without transaction or tax costs.

Figure 2. Returns of Top Dividend Paying Stocks in the S&P 500, 1957-2010

Since 1972, companies that increased or started paying dividends have returned 9.5% yearly, on average. In 19 of the past 20 years, S&P data show that dividend payers' shares did better than non-payers. [2]

How to Select a Stock

We are looking for shares of publicly traded companies that pay out some portion of their net income as dividends. Net income is income after all expenses have been paid: fixed and variable expenses, taxes, debt coverage, capital expenditures, and compensation. That disbursement can be in the form dividends. Growth in the value of that stock—commonly referred to as capital gain—is of secondary importance. We are going to live off of the income generated by the portfolio, some of which will be in the form of dividends. Income is real. It comes to us in the form of a check. We can cash that check. While this income does remain a promise—as a portion of profits earned—it is more than a prayer. As a dividend, the income is ours. We can take it and spend it for our comfortable retirement lifestyle.

Dividends should come from the actual earnings of the firm. If the company has to borrow in the capital markets or issue new stock to pay the dividend, we ignore that stock. It should come from free cash flow.[5] For example, let's say a firm earns $100 in profits. Its expenses are cost of goods, salaries, rent, and variable expenses such as marketing—perhaps totaling $50. The company has a net income of $50. If it decides to pay $10 out to its shareholders as a dividend, that is what we want to receive. While simple in the extreme, this is in essence what a profit and loss statement will tell us.

> **We are looking for shares of publicly traded companies that pay out some portion of their net income as dividends.**

How do we judge a stock? Dividend yield is a starting point, but not an evaluation tool. It simply tells us what the rate of dividend is based upon the current price. That "yield" changes with the stock price change. The yield is a function of a fleeting number. The price of the stock will change for any number of reasons. Some have to do with the company and are important: sales, profits, competitive advantage. Other reasons have to do with the industry (demand), the economy (growth, recession) or exogenous events (war, weather, terrorism).

We would like something more substantial than dividend yield. We'd like information about the current and future prospects for the company's ability to continue to pay the dividend. Since divi-

..ds are paid from surplus capital, we can observe the changes in
..is surplus as a trend. We can see what use senior management
makes of the surplus.

An excellent measure of a firm's ability to sustain dividends is
the payout ratio:

$$\frac{\text{Dividends}}{\text{Net Income minus Preferred Dividend}} = \text{Payout Ratio}$$

This compares the dividend to the net sales, less what may be
paid to the preferred shareholders. The number is a percentage
and will change over time.

Another of the older ideas is the P/B ratio: the comparison of price
to the book value for a firm. When you combine a search for higher
dividends and lower P/Bs, you tend toward firms whose total return[6]
may be higher and whose volatility is often lower.

Another quaint idea from an earlier time is the amount of debt
carried by the firm. The more interest a firm has to pay out of
gross income, the less net is left for dividends. We'd like to know
that the firm is wise about controlling its use of debt. It should
use an amount appropriate for its industry and capital position.
Debt is not necessarily bad. Excessively debt laden firms will suffer when interest rates rise. The cost of their debt can rise. This
increased "carry cost" will quickly drain surplus revenue, reduce
net income, and threaten the dividend payment.

Debt in excess of the equity value of the company is typically a
warning sign. Heed it as you would excessive debt on your family's
balance sheet. It easily becomes an indication of addiction. Excessive debt is to be avoided, particularly with small or mid-sized
enterprises. All firms need to borrow to grow, yes. Small cap firms

typically do not pay dividends. Our emphasis is on companies less growth oriented, more comfortable with sharing their excess returns with the stakeholders.[7]

It is not the intent of this book to discuss the many stock picking techniques outstanding or to educate the reader in the myriad ways of securities analysis. Should you need this education, you would do well to read the writings of Graham, Dodd, and Siegel. *The Intelligent Investor* and *Security Analysis* and are the best places to start. Follow that with Dr. Siegel's *Stocks for the Long Run*. These basic investment tomes are the fertile ground for the approaches described in this book.

> Since 1972, companies that increased or started paying dividends have returned 9.5% yearly, on average. In 19 of the past 20 years, S&P data show that payers' shares did better than non-payers' shares.
>
> —Ned Davis Research, 11/09

We have been discussing value investing. Value investing is straightforward. You own a company, not a stock. Ideally, you buy a company whose price is lower than its intrinsic value. The value is, essentially, the difference between its current assets and its debt. If the company has sufficient sales of its product or service to cover its operating overhead, its debt load, and pay a good dividend to its shareholders, then it qualifies for consideration.

A company that shares its wealth with its shareholders has a fair sense of the business and its prospects. Senior management is so comfortable with the firm's balance sheet that they can share the fruits of the company's labor with the public. There are no questionable footnotes to a dividend check sent to the shareholder of record, no FASB oddities, no earnings surprises. "The ability to pay and grow a dividend tells you about predictable, stable profits, balance sheets in good condition, even a well-protected franchise—all without the aid of inside numbers," says Don Kilbride of Vanguard Dividend Growth Fund (VDIGX). It really is just that simple.

Losses Are a Part of the Investment Process

The three time-honored criteria for choosing stocks—selecting companies that pay out decent dividends, have low price-to-book ratios, and carry low debt—offer little assurance of fail-safe returns. While owning a combination of stocks and bonds does help, there is no formula to prevent losses in your portfolio when you take risks.

Accept that fact. You should expect to fail. You should be prepared for losses. You can, however, minimize these losses by using a fourth time-honored approach: the stop loss. You set a price for a security, lower than what you paid. The simplest is a 10% loss. If the stock price falls to this point, you walk away. You accept the loss and turn your back. You go to the stable and choose a new mount. This time you lose. As Dryden wrote, "I'm a little wounded, but I am not slain … I'll rise and fight again." You have a well maintained list of stocks that currently meet your criteria. When one fails, you sell it once it reaches its stop loss price and invest in another company.

Despite information universally promulgated, owning stocks over the long haul is no assurance of gain. Gain is a matter of the price you pay, when you pay it, why you own it, and when you sell it. Each of these responsibilities is yours. The mere act of owning a stock portfolio has nothing to do with its performance. The time over which you own the stock portfolio has very little to do with its performance. The price you pay for the stocks and what you sell them for somewhat affects the portfolio performance.

There is a significant body of evidence indicating that we all make similar investment mistakes:

- We herd.
- We are overconfident.
- We assume expertise where randomness resides.
- We take success as an indicator of good judgment.
- We assume failure to be bad luck.

The "we" applies to all investors: institutional, mutual fund, and individual. We all put our pants on one leg at a time. We all make mistakes. Have you ever had your spouse suggest you may want to wear a different shirt? Your spouse was probably right—you made the wrong choice. Discount the advice of those who suggest that investment models are a means of overcoming these biases. A complex system is rarely in equilibrium and cannot be overridden by a rational system!

Failure is built into the genetic code of every living being. We are strengthened by failure, for we can learn from the experience. Putting your hand on a hot stove as a child is an enriching event—and one never repeated. You are designed to fail, repeatedly. Accept that fact as a given when investing. The trick is to both limit the failure harm (the burned hand) and to learn from the behavior (never touch a hot stove).

Going Deeper Than the Facts

Simply reading about a company and its stock price without interacting with its website, information office, or with other investors can result in a bias toward facts alone. Many subtleties do and should affect our decision making process. We ignore these subtleties at our peril.

If we were to examine the balance sheet of a firm such as ExxonMobil, our perspective will be colored by our accounting knowledge as well as our view towards energy extraction, the Exxon Valdez event, Prudhoe Bay, Exxon's dominance in the world of integrated oils, the current dividend and its history, the balance between profit sharing and capital expenditure, executive compensation, what we paid at the pump this afternoon, and a host of other factors. Do we have an opinion about peak oil? That opinion will change our view on the reserves accounting. Do we (dis)like drilling in Alaska? That viewpoint will impact what we think of the need to reserve capital. What about our "green" perspective?

These factors will change our attitude toward the firm. They are internal drivers that may have little or nothing to do with the facts of the case: the numbers on the balance sheet. They have everything to do with how we interpret those facts. Fifty people can easily arrive at 54 different opinions about the profit and loss statement! Large cap mutual fund managers can go on for hours about why Exxon is good, bad, or indifferent for their fund. They are counting angels on the head of a pin.[8]

The numbers from the P&L are the guidelines for the decision—they are not the decision itself. We buy a stock because we expect the price we pay to be less than or equal to the present value of the expected future dividends. Yet, we are also making a personal decision to accept the risk of ownership during the time of receipt of those distributions. It is not just about the math.

When selecting a company to invest in, ask pertinent questions: How does it work? What are its parts? Who makes decisions? What is the historical data? Why do you want it? How, when, and why can the company go wrong? The answers to these questions will provide you with information. Then you have to make a decision, for yourself. How you make that decision is based not only upon the facts you have gathered, but also upon the totality of experience you bring to the process. Buying stock is a subjective decision based upon objective facts.

You choose an investment because all of the information you gather is appropriate and substantial. You make the purchase because the investment makes sense to you. You do not choose it because the facts speak for themselves! You make a conscious act to accept the risk of ownership in anticipation of the reward of ownership. The stock purchase is your responsibility. The net income and dividend yield are metrics, they are not decision markers. They indicate distinctions among the competition; they do not define the choice. If investors make decisions based upon metrics, then they are condemning themselves to mediocrity. Many do so. A few investors stand out. Hopefully, you are a standout. Set your own standards. Apply them wisely. Make informed decisions. Know you will occasionally fail. Have a stable to back you up. Learn from others.

The Truth about Transaction Costs

Let's address the standard complaint that investing in individual stocks generates significant transaction costs. What impact could these costs have on the distribution rate of the hypothetical portfolio we are discussing? There are at least three answers to this query.

First, a value stock portfolio tends to be low transaction oriented. Once the ingredients are in place, the potential for change is minimal. You are not going to flip the portfolio. You are not going to incur internal expenses, as mutual funds may incur. You are only going to sell a stock if it drops below a particular point, initially 10% less than you paid for it.

The stock side of your value portfolio will certainly have more volatility than the bond side, which we'll discuss in the next chapter. You will incur an acquisition and disposal cost for stocks, as you will with bonds. If you own 12 to 15 stocks in the portfolio, you may reasonably expect one to three to break through their stop loss each year. This forces you to at least consider selling the stock and turn to your inventory for a replacement.

Under reasonable circumstances you can expect a low turnover portfolio to have very low expenses: .138% annual turnover costs. This compares quite favorably, by the way, with the lowest cost ETFs—the Vanguards of the world.

Stock Appreciation:
Reasonable Income, Organic Growth

You may be delighted to find your stocks appreciate in price over time. One of the classic assumptions regarding dividend paying stocks is that they are value stocks. As such, they display both low volatility and reasonable price definition.[9] You may deduce that their price will rise, since they are currently undervalued. The long-term holding of a dividend paying stock may, in many circumstances, lead to price appreciation. As investment strategist Jason Trennert has said, "There is ample evidence that companies with high payout ratios have grown earnings faster than those who choose to retain earnings for potential future growth opportunities."

For example, suppose you bought a stock for $25 and its value increased $5—to $30—over the next year. During this time you earned $1 in dividends. Your total annual return would be $6 or 24% on your original $25 investment. That's 4% higher than your return would have been for a non-dividend paying investment.

Many value investors hope to fully recoup the cost of acquisition from a value stock over several years just from the quarterly dividends. A stock paying a 5% dividend will recoup its price in 20 years; one paying a 10% will recoup its price in 10 years.

The negative costs associated with these portfolio types are minimal, by design. The positive costs may be a future joy: growth. We should not count on it, if the performance of the overall markets over the past two decades is any indication. We do not plan on it for our retirement income needs, as do many planning experts.[10] If growth happens, we are pleased. Ideally, it may increase the value of our portfolio to keep pace with inflation. If this potential increase allows us to make gifts to grandchildren or trips to visit them, fine. Growth is a secondary characteristic of our design process rather than a necessary condition. Reliance upon growth has repeatedly led to disaster for many portfolios—from the individual's portfolio to the institutional fund's portfolio. In fact, the mutual fund industry can be called "the pathway to mediocrity."

Narrowing Down the Winners

How do individual investors find stocks that meet their value oriented criteria? One way is to peruse investment websites such as FINVIZ.com, dividendinvestor.com, or quantumonline.com.

An even better method of narrowing down winners is to screen for companies that meet your criteria. We can set filters to describe what we want to see in a company:

- We like net income because that legitimately allows for dividends.
- Free cash flow is one measure of real net income.
- We like to know that debt is reasonable, if the firm needs to use debt.

- We'd like to see that some of the net income is used for dividend payments—but not all or more than all of that net income.
- We would love to know that the company has been paying the dividends for some time. Ideally, it has been increasing the dividends each year.

In August of 2010, using the website FINVIZ.com, we discover that more than 10% (618) of the entire US market of stock (57,544) listings[11] today offer dividends in excess of 6% (including ETFs). Nearly half of the US market pays dividends (2,817)[12] of more than .1%. Of the stocks that do pay dividends in excess of 6%, 111 have debt-to-equity ratios lower than 90%. We can further narrow down our stock selection screen by filtering for average trading volume of over 50,000 shares daily, which gives us a group of 66.[13] You can screen for any of dozens of sets and subsets of data beyond here.

The results are a small group of stocks that meet your criteria. At the website FINVIZ.com you have made choices such as US or foreign, dividend yield, debt-to-equity ratio, and average trading volume. The size and composition of the list will change with time. You can choose any criteria you wish from their 55 variables. Think of this as your stable of horses. As you look further into the details of each firm you will ultimately choose a small group that will support your income needs and meet your financial criteria.

Remember that the stock market is dynamic. This list will change with time. Revisit and renew your list at least each quarter. The types, sizes, dividends, and number of firms on the list are in constant flux. This flux is either because the price has changed— to the advantage or disadvantage of the shareholders—or because other factors have moved the firms across the lists.

Once you create this list, you will see that it reveals a fairly wide selection of styles[14], sizes, and sectors from which to choose. In October of 2010, large caps were represented by six firms. There were 21 midcap, 24 small cap, and 15 microcap stocks. Industries are as follows:

Property & Casualty Insurers	4
REITs	18
Oil/gas/explore/refine/trans	16
Insurance	1
Banks	5
Telecoms	2
Consumer Goods	1
Consumer Services	2
Brokerages	2
BDCs	15

Market sectors are:

Financial	45
Basic Materials	16
Consumer Services	2
Consumer Goods	1
Technology	2

However you slice and dice, there is a reasonably wide variety of products and services offered by these companies that pay dividends.

In the large cap world we have two telecoms, a BDC, a REIT, a consumer goods, and a pipeline partnership MLP. For purposes of example, let's examine the telecom, Centurytel (CTL).

Centurytel is based in Monroe, LA and was founded in 1968 as part of the Bell spinoff. It provides integrated telecommunications services in 33 states. They control more than 70% of the voice/data transmissions over their own network. Its broadband penetration rate of 88% is among the highest of their peer group. They have low debt, outstanding positioning in the credit markets, deep and wide penetration of their customer markets which continually expand, are regarded as excellent cost managers and thus have significant operations margins and free cash flow. Over the past 15 years they have outperformed the S&P Telecom Index by three fold, a noteworthy statement. Their strength is witnessed by their sustained dividend payout. For 36 years they have paid a dividend.

Thirty-six years of dividend increases is an impressive series. Over the past five years those dividend increases have averaged 63%. A debt-to-equity ratio of less than 90% with a market capitalization of $10 billion is well done. CTL has a five-year total return of nearly 20% during the worst market value destruction in a generation. You can sleep well with these kinds of numbers. Always vigilant, of course—past performance is no indication of future success.

A Word about Preferred Stock

One of the oldest and easiest investments to make is that of a preferred stock. It stands in preference to common in terms of dividend distribution. Preferreds pay a dividend that is senior to common stock dividends and secondary to any debt. While this sounds attractive, they offer little or no upside, except in cases of extreme market turmoil, such as 2008-09. They can have thinly traded markets, which may result in a substantial difference between the price you pay for the stock and what you might be forced to sell it for. The vast majority are linked to financial companies and share their volatility, without sharing in their upside. Plus, you have no voting rights.[15]

For these reasons, your use of preferreds should not exceed 15% of your portfolio. You should only use traditional cumulative preferred stock. They should be acquired only when their price is depressed—and depressed for a market reason, not because the stock has been faced with a challenge. Educate yourself before investing.

Summary

Owning a portfolio of individual stocks can be an excellent way to populate your retirement portfolio, provided that you use the basic tools of the savvy value stock investor:

+ Search out sustainable dividends paid reliably for many years. Invest in firms with low price-to-book ratios.
+ Invest in firms with low debt. Some debt can be good; excessive debt is bad.
+ Volume matters when you need to execute your sell order(s). Search out firms with market strength.
+ Stop loss each position.

While the above are time-tested tools, be advised: from time to time they will fail, as do all tools. When one fails, try another tool. Don't keep using a broken tool, you will only hurt yourself. Remember:

There are no perfect sets of rules
that apply in every situation.

Anyone who tells you—for a small fee—that their investment idea will make you millions is misleading you so that they can pay for their yacht! *Caveat emptor.*

Finally, remember that while there is no guarantee that your stock portfolio will return 7% over time, it's a near certainty that your cash investments will not do so. For further ideas on how to build your 7% portfolio, let us turn to the next chapter on bonds.

WORKSHEET

Assignments:

1. Visit FINVIZ.com. Explore and learn. Take your time.

2. Visit quantumonline.com. Do the same. The learning process for many of you will be long and steep. This is like visiting a new bookstore. Enjoy.

3. Google "Benjamin Graham." Read and learn. Do the same for "Charles Munger" and "Dr. Jeremy Seigel."

4. Take notes about what is important to you.

6

EMBRACING BONDS

The great and mysterious Bondworld. What is it? Who knows its arcane rules? How can we ever penetrate its mystery? Where do we enter its labyrinthine passageways? When can we exit the mysterious cave? Why should mere mortals attempt this desperate plight?

We have for five generations followed the meanderings of the stock market. We attempt to discover its secrets with incantations, with ritual, with secret formulae available only to the fortunate—for a small price, billable to your credit card. We are fascinated by its complexity. To it we subscribe vast resources, pen mighty tomes, converse with the anointed.

The bond market we leave to the mystics. We will buy the typical bond mutual fund and accept their tremulous safety. We grimace when they collapse every so often—1982, 1987, 1994, 1997, 2004, 2007. We pay their outrageous fees, accept their mediocre returns. Why? Because we are fearful of entering the maze. The Minotaur lies in wait, certainly. Death is in store—by a thousand rate increases, by inflation's mighty sword, by bankruptcy courts fleecing the debt holder. Tremble all, ye who enter here. If you think stocks are confusing, common wisdom seems to say, take a look at bonds.

The Truth about Bonds

Actually, bonds are just as straightforward as any stock, easier in many cases. The fears extolled of interest rate changes, inflation, and bankruptcies are put to rest by an examination of the facts and circumstances. You can manage these risks more effectively through the purchase of individual bonds than you can with a bond mutual fund. You can effectively take advantage of their fluctuations by the simple tool of laddering.

Your greatest enemy may lie within your current portfolio—the bond mutual fund. If ever there were a culprit, it is the bond mutual fund. You are simultaneously giving up yield and increasing risk with its use. The fees charged take directly from your yield. Their massive size exaggerates the effects of inflation and of interest rate increases. You use bond funds because you do not understand the world of bonds. The Wizard has fooled you. He is building a huge home in Newport Beach, California, with the proceeds of your foolish fears. Many wish to employ him and his cohorts. So be it. If you choose, you may fire him. He is not a bad man. He is not evil. He is there for the uninformed—those who don't know better—or for the lazy—for those who won't do the work. It does appear odd that large institutional firms pay very low annual fees to bond fund advisors, typically .15 to .28, while we pay fees of .55 to .95. One can only wonder at the pricing cost differential. Large investors have far greater access for a far lower cost. Hmm. Does the paperwork and tracking of individual accounts really cost that much?

Income during retirement—this is what we each search for; that is what we each need in our portfolios. After fixed assets like bank deposits, CDs, money market funds, and savings accounts, the wide panorama of bonds is a major area of relatively safe income—as long as you invest wisely. This is the world of debt. It is inhabited by individual grazers (that would be you) and larger herds of institutional feeders. We all come for the relative safety of the income stream issuing from debt. Each of us has our own appetite for interest; each of us learns to take what we like and leave the rest for the others who feed here. As small animals on the vast grazing grounds of Bondworld, we do need to watch for the large herds.

Used correctly, bonds offer income, capital preservation, and reduced volatility in your portfolio. But very much like our stock friends, bonds carry risks as well as rewards. This chapter will serve as your guide to the bond market—how it functions, its potential risks, and how to invest in it with confidence.

What Are Bonds—and What Do They Offer?

Essentially, a bond is a loan—money lent either to the US government (called Treasuries), to US cities, states, and other municipalities (called tax-exempt municipals), or to corporations (called corporates). When you buy a bond, you are loaning money to the borrower. If the borrower repays at the end of the loan's full term, the bond is said to have "matured." If the borrower decides to pay the loan before maturity, the bond is said to have been "called."

Bonds offer two kinds of returns. First, returns include the income from the semi-annual interest payments over the life of the loan. Second, returns include any change in the market price of the bond. Here is a key fact about bonds: their market price is inversely affected by interest rates. If interest rates have risen since your bond was issued, your bond is worth less than it was when you bought it. If interest rates have fallen since your bond was issued, your bond is worth more than it was when you bought it. Keep in mind that while fluctuating interest rates will affect the market price of your bond, they will not affect the actual interest payments you get from your bond. Those interest payments will always remain the same. Interest rate changes will not affect the value of your investment in the bond as long as you hold it to maturity. The change in value will appear as such on your statement, but as long as you hold it until it matures, that is irrelevant information.

> **Here is a key fact about bonds: their market price is inversely affected by interest rates.**

For example, suppose you invested $10,000 in a bond paying 4% interest annually. Assume rates fall and new bonds now yield 3%. You would still earn 4%. If you had to sell your bond it would be worth more than $10,000, because the market value of a bond increases when interest rates fall. The reverse is true, as well. If interest rates increased to 5%, the bond would be worth less than $10,000.

Risks of Bond Ownership

The first, most obvious risk is stated in the previous paragraph—*inflationary risk*. This leads directly to its corollary: *market risk*. As rates change, as inflation changes, the value of bonds changes inversely. Knowing this core law of Bondworld will allow you to better prepare yourself.

The second form of risk is one of *quality*. Bonds are rated by various public and quasi-government agencies. The rating reflects the agencies' perspectives as to the bond's "soundness." We all know to take the word of any government official or agency with a very large grain of salt. The debacle of 2007-2009 was a direct result of ratings obscuring actual value, ratings being "bought" by issuers who buried garbage mortgages underneath tranches of better debt. These collateralized mortgage obligations (CMOs) and collateralized debt obligations (CDOs) are still being unraveled at significant cost to taxpayers.

Having said that, most bonds issued are single purpose, rather than those complex creatures of investment banks which precipitated the recent capital markets crash. Ratings vary from AAA through AA, A, BBB, BB, B, CCC, CC, C, and D. Just as in school, the lower the letter, the worse the grade. For retirement income, we want to focus upon only bonds with grades of AAA to BBB. These are institutional and investment grade bonds. Their historical default rates are less than 3%. As a whole, 97% of this section of the bond market has always repaid interest and capital. If you note a significant difference in yields between two bonds of similar quality, something is amiss with one. Investigate further before buying.

The third type of risk is *issuer risk*. This is far more important to the junk world of BB to D bonds. As retirees, we usually do not want to play in this arena. The exception might be during good economic times, when you might have as much as 10% of the bond portion of your portfolio in BB.

Issuer risk is very important when you buy municipal bonds. GO, or general obligation, bonds have the "full fair and credit" of the issuing government behind them. Their yields are typically lower than revenue bonds and are supported from a specific source of income—for example, a water or school district—or tobacco bonds. Servicing the bond—paying you interest every six months—is the source and the risk of these bonds. These bonds may be education, entertainment, health care, transportation, housing, or utility supported. At these levels of investment, you want to be very interested in doing your homework. Tax exempt revenue bonds require much research and understanding. You and your bond desk have to have a strong relationship. You have to be an informed investor to play here.

Another risk is *call risk*. A bond issuer may retain the right to call the bond if interest rates have so moved that the balance sheet would be positively affected by calling the older, higher interest rate bond and re-issuing a new bond at a lower rate. You do need to pay close attention to the call date if a bond has one. You do not want to pay more than the call price and you want to know the YTC—yield to call calculation.

Systemic risks can be political, event, or tax policy based. Any of these can lead to liquidity risk for the markets themselves, as we saw in late 2008. You cannot manage this risk effectively, but you do need to be aware of it. For example, were fiscal policy to change to a flat tax policy, the municipal bond market would undergo a complex systemic risk. If a global conflict arose, the bond markets would suffer systemic risk. Minor or major changes at the local and national political levels can impact a single bond or the market as a whole.

Finally, *liquidity risk* can occur at the level of the individual bond, at a sector level, or at the whole system level. If most of a bond offering is taken by an institution on offering date, the remaining amount can be very thinly traded. This is liquidity risk.

A particular industry or city may be at risk, reducing the liquidity of bonds so issued. Systemic risk will rip through the fabric of the entire market, as did the liquidity crisis of September 2008, when even banks were afraid to lend over one night.

Mastering Bondspeak

Before grazing in the bond fields, it's best to become conversant in Bondspeak. The following terms describe the various aspects of bonds.

Coupon. This is the interest payment you will receive—the old "coupon" we used to clip before electrons took the task away from us. Coupons are typically paid out every six months. Using our earlier example, a $10,000 bond paying 4% interest has a $400 annual coupon, or $200 paid semiannually.

Current Yield: This is the annual interest rate divided by the price you have paid for the bond. In our example, the new issue, $10,000 bond paying $400 a year has a current yield of 4%.

Death put option: This is an optional feature on some bonds that allows your heir to sell (put) the bond back to the issuer and receive its face value (the amount paid at its maturity date), should you pass away during the lifetime of the bond. This applies to bank CDs, agency notes, and both corporate and mortgage backed notes established for individual buyers. These are unusual; you have to look for them, you have to ask for them. They can have value during a time of rising interest rates, when bond prices are declining. They can offer significant value to your estate. Few bonds have this call option. Ask for bonds with it when you shop.

Market value: This is what your bond is worth in the current market. Again, if interest rates have fallen since the bond was issued, your bond will have greater market value. Conversely, if interest rates have risen, your bond will have less market value. This will change daily, but in very minor amounts. At the investment and institutional grade levels, we can effectively ignore it.

Rating. As stated above, bonds are rated from AAA (outstanding) to D (defaulted), from one of the agencies whose task it is to describe their components and risks. Again, as with all sources of information, take these ratings with a grain of salt. The ratings reports are backwards looking—a rearview mirror of what the perspective on the bond was when it was issued. For example, a municipal rated AAA in the 1990s might not be so stellar today. You also need to know if the rating has changed or is under watch—not that this will guide you, other than away from any watch listed bond. You do want to be aware if any rating change has happened to one of the bonds in your portfolio.

Term: This is the lifespan of the bond. Short-term bonds run from 30 days to one year. Intermediate term bonds live up to ten years. Long-term bonds live even longer than that. A long-term Treasury bond, for example, typically has a term of 30 years, sometimes even longer. There are 100-year bonds.

Total return: This is the number to pay attention to. It is determined by all the interest you received over the life of the bond and the bond's gain or loss in market value.

Yield to call: This is the yield to the first call date. As discussed above, many bonds have a call feature. The "make whole" call allows the issuer to call a bond at the time of its choosing by paying face value plus a nominal premium, typically 1% to 2%. Companies can—and should—do so when interest rates have declined to the point where the reissuance at a lower rate makes sense. If the company has debt and also pays a dividend, then by lowering its interest rate charged against earnings, the dividend becomes both more secure and more valuable.

Yield to maturity: This is the yield you will receive assuming you hold your bond to maturity and it includes any capital gain or loss based upon your purchase price. This is the benchmark against which bonds are traded. Yield to maturity (YTM) is the ultimate determinate of the value of your investment. You will be receiving the coupon paid every six months from the bond issuer, to your account. If you bought the bond for less than face value, you will also receive the appreciation to par when it matures. This concept is a key to your understanding of investing in the bond market. You are looking for coupon and for appreciation. The appreciation will usually be small, 1 to 3%, but it will be a pleasant reminder of your prowess.

Yield to worst: This is the yield you will receive if the bond is called early.

Understanding the Bond Markets

As we hinted earlier, Bondworld is complex. Stockworld is complex. This means you want to approach both domains with knowledge and strength. The following describes the broad categories of bonds. Within each category a variety of choices reside.

Government Bonds: These are essentially an IOU from the United States government. They include Treasury bills, notes, and bonds, as well as agency debt.

Corporate Bonds: These are essentially loans to corporations. They come in varying qualities: institutional quality, investment grade, medium term notes (MTNs), and junk.

Municipals: Issued by a state, municipality, or county to finance public projects, these bonds are generally exempt from federal taxes and from most state and local taxes. Interest income may be subject to the alternative minimum tax.

Foreign (non-US) Bonds: These are issued in a domestic market by a foreign entity, in the domestic market's currency. They include sovereign debt and foreign corporate bonds. International investing involves special risks such as currency fluctuation and political instability and may not be suitable for all investors.

Zero Coupon Bonds: These are issued at a discount to their face value and rise in value each year as they approach maturity. Zero coupon bonds are subject to large price fluctuations if sold prior to maturity. They do not pay interest; they accrue value. They can be issued by any of the above entities. As we are trying to live on the interest from bonds, these are rarely part of our portfolio.

Before jumping into researching and buying bonds for your value portfolio, it will serve you well to gain an understanding of the overall bond market.

The bond markets are huge—far, far larger than their corresponding stock markets. In Bondworld, the big players dominate the field. They are institutional: pensions, life insurance companies, mutual funds. They are investment banks: Goldman Sachs, Merrill, Credit Suisse, etc. They are hedge funds, who often look to make money on the spread between interest rates and market value. Their time horizons are usually very short, yet their immense size can force—and take advantage of—market distortions. These players are very much like gravity sinks in cosmology. They can distort the field of Bondworld space and time. In 1997, the huge hedge fund LTCM did just this, ripping the fabric of the global markets.[1]

The first group, pensions and life insurers, typically invests for the long term. They buy and hold bonds to maturity. Rarely do they sell out from their accounts. Because of their voracious appetites—they can take all of a $1 billion issue without blinking—pensions can reduce the liquidity in a market for some bonds by owning the vast majority of an issue. Reduced liquidity quickly becomes marked up in the buy or sell transaction, which means you may pay a higher price.

The second group, investment banks, brings bonds to the marketplace and gets paid a fee for so doing. They often take a portion of the newly issued bond to hold for their own portfolios or for their inventory, to later mark up and sell to retail and wholesale customers. That would be you. Again, the mark up is part of what you pay and it affects the return you receive. They can also be market makers, dealers who buy and sell in the open market, thus providing liquidity for the issue. They charge a price for this, certainly. It is a price well paid. Without liquidity at the retail level, we would be subject to the whims of the institutions.

The third group, mutual funds, has little if any interaction on your level of play in the bond field. Yet, it can have an inordinate impact upon the field itself—and upon the value and liquidity of your bond portfolio.

Hedge funds play a directional game. They look for a move, trying to ride and influence it to their advantage. The move's direction is immaterial to them, hence the danger. They can just as easily make a profit riding the roller coaster of interest rates down as they can riding it up. They are agnostic, while you are ecclesiastic.

The first challenge these herds present is size. We want to graze in the rich fields for bond income, while not being grazed by the larger beasties. Pensions, life insurance companies, and mutual funds can overpower a market or an issue by contributing to or taking away demand. Markets are best when the relationship between supply and demand is elastic. When it is sticky, pricing discrepancies appear. While hedge funds desire stickiness, pension fund and insurers ignore it, and mutual fund accounts get hammered by it. If you have to enter the market at such a time, the stickiness is not to your advantage.

The second challenge is liquidity. These beasts can consume an issue or series of issues between them. They can take 90% of a $500 million offering, leaving only $50 million for retail investors. What appears to be a sizeable market for the issue is actually a very small market, which can easily translate into a higher price for you. The big players can also withhold liquidity from a market by refusing to buy or sell. If a bond has a call feature, their position may be so large that their tender defines the result, whether or not you wish to participate. They can influence the ratings agencies—and have for some time—to grade an issue differently than its components parts would indicate. A recent painful example: most of the mortgage-backed securities—the aforementioned CMOs and CDOs—were falsely graded institutional grade, despite the lesser value of the myriad mortgages within.

The third challenge is regulatory. The size of these beasts invites oversight by government agencies. No matter what your political persuasion, regulatory involvement adds cost and reduces liquidity—the opposite of what is expected. The cost may be as simple as taxation of the interest, or as complex as an imbedded fee structure or the requirement to send prospectuses to investors regularly.

Taxation of the interest received from bonds can be onerous or generous to you. Municipals are often tax free, except for the new Build America Bonds (BABs). Govvies, government bonds, international bonds, and most US Treasury bonds are taxable.

If you have the luxury of choice, you may prefer to hold taxable bonds in your retirement account, thus deferring taxation until withdrawal. BABs and munis are held in your personal account. If you have zero coupon bonds, they may best be held in your retirement account—otherwise you can pay taxes on income you do not receive!

Finding the Right Bonds for Your Value Portfolio

Despite the challenges presented by the bond beasts, the bond fields offer dependable sustenance for the value investor. But where do we find information about bonds and how do we evaluate them?

The web gives us a panoply of resources. SIMFA, FINRA, NASDAQ, and the SEC are excellent guideposts. You will learn the facts. Let's begin at the SIMFA site. Observe the bond markets in action at investinginbonds.com. Here you will see the trading in the bond market. Here you will begin your search for bonds that meet your income and risk choices. The learning process is rich and rewarding here. The FINRA.org site offers extensive detail and lessons in the market. Here you can input a bond's ID and learn where it fits in the issuer's debt structure—the "capital stack." You can learn more about the firm or the government that created the bond, the views of the agencies, and the activities of major players with the bond.

Your investment firm's research department is the next stop—or your financial advisor. Here you will discover current availability and pricing. You want to establish a strong rapport with the FI (fixed income) desk, or assure yourself that your advisor has such a relationship. What you ultimately pay for each bond will directly impact your portfolio's return.

How to Buy Bonds

Buying bonds can be a reasonable "day at the fair." You will seek what you need, discover prices for what is available from the vendors, negotiate prices with them, and take your basket home. Once you have created your bond portfolio, you may only need to return to the market once a year, to replace a bond that has matured. As bond prices change so slowly and as you have bought these to hold until maturity, the process of acquiring and tracking bonds is far less laborious than that of stocks.

Having watched the market for a bond, you will know the current prices others have paid. You will then dictate the price you are willing to pay for the bond you have chosen. The desk will make every good effort to fill your order, or come back to you with another price. You may be buying from the inventory at the desk or from another source with which they work. The "markup" is the price you pay for the transaction. You want the desk to tell you what the effective yield will be to you for the markup, or do the simple calculation for yourself. If the cost is reasonable, you will proceed with the purchase. If not, you may offer another price, or look for another bond if the seller will not budge on price.

Take your time. During the course of shopping at investinginbonds.com or from your firm's inventory, you may find a dozen interesting choices. You may ultimately buy only one or two of those bonds. Availability, pricing, and size will affect your shopping cart. Remember, once you have bought the bond, you will be holding it for a number of years. Buy wisely.

The price of an individual bond depends only upon your stated price—what you are willing to pay Mr. Market. In most cases, we will try to pay less than face value for a bond, thus earning some amount of appreciation. This appreciation is icing on the cake, the interest being the cake!

Some investors fear corporate bonds. What if the management changes, what if there's a takeover attempt, what if, what if, what if? While it's true that buying a corporate bond essentially means that you are taking on the risk of that company, it's worthwhile to know that less than 3% of all investment grade corporate bonds issued have defaulted. Your well researched bond will have an even lower default rate. You will still apply the 10% stop loss rule to your bonds. During the recession of 2008, GM bonds began to show the impact of reduced auto purchases by the public. They dropped in value, as did the GMAC bonds. Had you been invested in GM and applied our 10% stop loss rule, you would have had to walk away from the GM bonds you owned in 2008. As a result, you fortunately would not have participated in the debacle of the government takeover of the company in early 2009 that resulted in devastation to the bondholders.

High-yield junk bonds are usually to be avoided by the conservative, astute investor. The yield differential is rarely worth the price of capital risk.[2]

Yields available across Bondworld will be determined by the quality of the bond issuer, the amount of other debt the issuer has, the duration of the bond, the current economic environment, and fiscal and monetary policy currently in effect. Your need for retirement income will dictate the yield you need from the bond portion of your portfolio. Expectations of a 6% yield from your bond portfolio are, in most times, reasonable. You may find those yields from any of the corporate, government, international, or global bond markets.

Climbing the Bond Ladder

The ideal strategy for buying income producing bonds is to purchase a group of bonds with varying maturities. You will stagger your purchases across time. This is called laddering. You will manage *duration risk* with this strategy. You are going to turn in each bond at maturity and replace it with another. If you have eight bonds with staggering maturities over eight years, you will buy a bond once a year. Each year, as a bond matures, you will reinvest those proceeds into a new bond, striving to maintain your 6% bond yield. Duration is the length of time until maturity of each bond. You will shorten or lengthen the duration of each bond acquisition according to: first, your income need and second, your perception of the bond world. For example, if you have $80,000 maturing and you still need the $2,400 semi-annual payment, you then look to the market for yield, quality, duration, and price—in that order.

Acquiring each unit, and ultimately disposing of it, will have a cost. If you hold that unit for a period of time, the acquisition and disposal fee has to be amortized over that time. We'll discuss the details of bond purchasing strategy in Chapter 11, "Designing the 7% Portfolio."

Lessons from History

The history of the bond market provides many valuable lessons for the savvy investor.[3] For our purposes, we are interested in picking up the story in the last quarter of the 20th century. When inflation became the brute of the late seventies, interest rates rose appallingly. As you will recall, bank CD rates of 15% for five years were normal during those "gas line" years. Bonds—whose values decline as interest rates rise—were decimated. Between 1978 and 1982, interest rates rose and bond values plummeted. Common wisdom was that the bond market was a slaughterhouse of the innocent at the hands of Wall Street.

The 1980s gave bonds their best decade for returns ever. According to a study from Salomon Brothers, bonds were the most profitable place to store wealth, averaging a return of 20.9%.[4]

Stocks, so enamored by the media, had a return of 16.5% in the same decade, one of their best ever. The phrase "buy when blood runs in the Street" comes to mind.[5]

Bonds are the best supporting actors in your retirement portfolio. If you purchase a well-researched mix of intermediate bonds and live off the interest each year, your capital can be well nourished in the rich fields of bond income.

WORKSHEET

Assignment: Explore helpful websites.

1. Visit the following websites. Spend as much time as you can at each site, learning, discovering, and experimenting. Subscribe to those that interest you.

    Investinginbonds.com
    Quantumonline.com
    Finra.org
    Sifma.org
    Emma.msrb.org
    Bondsonline.com

2. Acquire and begin reading *Bonds* by Hildy Richelson.

7

EXPLORING LOW MAINTENANCE INVESTMENTS: MUTUAL FUNDS, ETFS, AND CEFS

"Past performance is no indication of future results."
—Ubiquitous financial statement legalese

So far we've talked about the possibility of replacing your underperforming mutual funds with a selection of dividend paying stocks and laddering your bonds in an effort to earn as much as 7% in your portfolio. These tasks will require only a modest amount of your time. Nevertheless, if this strikes you as too much work—you'd rather spend your time enjoying the grandkids—other investment vehicles are available. We'll explore three of them here: mutual funds, electronically traded funds (ETFs) and closed end funds (CEFs).

Warning: After reading this chapter, you might not be so complacent about dumping your retirement portfolio into mutual funds so that you can enjoy the "convenience" of diversification and passive portfolio management. We've already touched on the downside of over-diversification and following the lemming-like herd. In this chapter we'll explore the real costs of owning mutual funds. Vanguard founder and retired CEO John Bogle is correct: the lower the cost, the more you keep. It really is that simple.

Ultimately it is the market—not the manager—that dictates the performance of the fund. Ignore that observation at your own risk. If you are unwilling to do the work of maintaining your own stock and bond portfolio, then use a mutual fund with low expenses, and one that closely reflects the index against which it is measured.

MUTUAL FUNDS

The vast majority of investors today use mutual funds. We don't need to explain their mechanics and application to your portfolio here. You know how they work and how you employ them in your portfolio. Suffice it to say that a fund is a collection of securities chosen for a reason and treated as a member of a larger group. How they are selected and used is a function of the design of the particular fund. There are thousands of funds. Their total assets exceeded $12 trillion in 2010. There are bond, stock, alternative, and combinations of these three categories. Their variety appears endless.[1]

As with any large capital purchase, you may want to look under the hood before investing in a fund. What are its costs? How is it structured? How does this investment compare to others?

Survivorship Bias

When comparing investments, keep in mind that mutual funds come and go with abnormal frequency. This leads to survivorship bias, of which you should be wary. When a group of funds are described as "beating the market," you have to ask, "What group?"

You might hear that over a ten-year period 30% of all mutual funds outperformed the S&P 500. Look beneath the sheets. Over that time frame many funds went out of business or merged with a cousin. If you track all funds that were around at the beginning of this decade and compared all returns, the 30% number of out-performers would drop significantly.

The surviving funds tend to be slightly better at what they do (taking your money). The numbers you are offered through their prospectuses and advertising may ignore the losers and reward the winners and the middle-of-the-pack survivors. This is also known as cherry picking, data mining, and setting the table. It is less than truthful at best. Fees earned by the mutual fund industry in 2009 (a rather bad year) were more than $109 billion! *Caveat emptor:* Let the buyer beware.

Costs of Ownership

According to the SEC website, there are several types of mutual fund fees and expenses: sales loads (current or deferred), redemption fees, exchange fees, account fees, purchase fees, management fees, distribution fees, other expenses, and operating expenses. No one fund has all of these fees. No one fund is without some of these fees. At the investment level there are more expenses: transaction charges, spread costs, trading costs, allocation expenses. At the investor level the costs include short- and long-term tax expenses, liquidity costs, survivorship bias, investor bias, and the price of fear and/or greed.

Costs associated with owning mutual fund shares are complex. Fund companies might make these costs readily obvious—or be less than virtuous in disclosing them.

Costs of ownership may include a *sales commission* to purchase shares. If you do incur a sales charge—commission—

then you need to be aware of break points. If you're investing $250,000, you do not want to put $50,000 into five different mutual fund companies if they each have similar break points and offer reasonably similar funds. Putting an entire $250,000 into a variety of funds in one company will mean a considerably lower commission cost. Too often a broker will use five different mutual fund companies because, presto, he is paid a commission on each buy. The less commission you pay, the less he receives. Very simple. Very devious. This occurs with obscene regularity. Members of FINRA should not sell shares just below a break point to earn higher commissions.

If you are keen to trade funds, then the fund company may impose an *exchange fee* for the event. They want a steady inflow of capital, rather than a disruptive outflow. If you insist upon trading the account, they may charge you for the privilege. This charge may be imposed for a period of time, perhaps 30 or 90 days.

A *purchase fee* may be imposed by the fund company. It directly reimburses the firm for its costs incurred in the creation, marketing, distribution, and maintenance of the fund shares.

Management fees are paid to the fund company's management team for the actual act of managing the investment. These would be salaries or wages, research costs, office overhead, and the like. These fees can be quite variable. The compensation paid to the fund manager can be determined in any number of complex ways. The most important tends to be "The Rule of Number One" in the mutual fund industry:

- Performance defines ranking.
- Ranking attracts capital.
- Capital earns revenue.
- Performance based pay follows from these precepts.

Remember, no fund manager earns his pay over the long term; a fund manager makes money by earning a percentage of the annual asset management fee. He is typically rewarded for bringing in assets, retaining assets under management, and managing expenses. He may be further compensated for meeting a target return, an index return, or beating an index.

As the size of a fund increases, you might expect the fees to decline, since they are taking the same percentage from a larger pie, and thus earning more for the same approximate cost. Yet in many funds there is no internal fee reduction as the fund grows larger. Often it is just the opposite: the fund increases its fees as it grows. Beware. Here is a quick example of how this applied in the time period 12/31/09 and 5/31/2010.

Fund Name	Size Change	Expense %	Expense Change
ABCDX	69%	.69%	+ 4.5%
EFGHX	55%	.43%	no change
IJKLX	300%	.57%	-10%
MNOPX	36%	1.25%	+3%
QRSTX	192%	1.08%	+5.6%

You can make up your own mind about these changes and charges. These events are not unusual. They are difficult to discover. You must do your work, even if you use mutual funds—especially if you use costly ones for the relatively simple world of bonds.

Distribution fees or *12b-1 fees* are those expenses incurred by the fund company for the distribution, marketing, and sales of fund shares. These include but are not limited to printing, mailing, marketing, and advertising. They cannot exceed .75% of a fund's average net assets each year.

Shareholder service fees may be authorized, as well, as much as .25% of the average net assets. These fees are for the statements you receive, the toll free phone you call, and the tax information sent to you at year end.

Other expenses can be *expenses not previously included, custodial fees, transfer fees, agency fees, legal fees, accounting fees*, and *other administrative expenses*. These are small individually, but can add up quickly, particularly if you have a small amount invested. For example, the custodial fee can be $12 to $100 a year for an IRA, with $30 as a typical annual fee. For a $2,000 investment, that can be an additional 1.5%; for $5,000 it is an additional .6% each year.

Trading costs—the expense of buying and selling a security—are not disclosed in the prospectus. They are fungible. They change each year and can be "offset" in a variety of ways. If a portion of an IPO is taken up by a fund company, it can allocate the shares acquired to any number of its mutual funds. If it does so to a smaller, newer fund and that allocation (and return) results in a significant increase in the fund's return, capital may be drawn to the new boy on the block. Trading expenses in general can average .78% each year of funds' net assets. Trading costs can be enhanced by the "trading" of research for fees. These deals may be at variance with a "best execution" ideal for trading. Of course, these expenses are often passed on to you, the shareholder, rather than paid for by the fund company.

Spread costs are the difference between the bid price (what a buyer will pay for a stock) and the ask price (the price at which the seller will sell). In large transactions, spread costs are nominal to virtually non-existent. For smaller trades, they can be significant. Suppose the spread for a stock is $24.15 (the bid price) and $24.32 (the ask price). That $.17 per share cost can be the difference between a sizeable gain and a fair gain. It depends upon the ability and agility of the desk trader to "make the spread" (buy at the bid price and sell at the ask price). If, because of his skill, experience, contacts, knowledge, and placement technique, he can execute between the spread, the shareholder and the fund wins. If he cannot, then a winner becomes an also ran. These costs can destroy a bond fund's returns, because the bond market remains so opaque. The spreads are still a gentlemen's agreement—and can be a reason to steal. Very few bond funds can overcome their expense bias.

Indirect Mutual Fund Expenses

These costs occur at your level of ownership, rather than at the mutual fund level, or occur because of market events than change the texture of the fund itself.

Taxes are due upon a gain that is realized and recognized in a non-qualified account, according to the Internal Revenue Service. Securities are purchased at a price. Later, those securities are sold. If the difference between these two prices is positive— if you have a gain—then taxes are due. If the holding period for the security is more than twelve months, the gain is taxed at the current long-term capital gains rate. If it was held for less than the requisite twelve months, the gain is taxed at the short-term capital gains rate. This rate is the same tax rate as ordinary income—your W-2 income.

Here is the problem. The holding period for most securities held by mutual funds is now less than four months. Why? Performance. The fund managers are rated upon their quarterly performance. It can be very enticing to juice the return with a short-term gain followed by a new acquisition and a new, unrealized yet recognized gain, particularly during bull markets. If you were a mutual fund manager who had three kids in college at $40,000 a year, a third wife, four cars, a house in the city, and another upstate, with an ailing new mother-in-law, would you be tempted to juice your compensation for a few quick stock sales? This results in higher taxes for you, the investor.

Liquidity costs can arise within a market. They can also arise within an investment. Regard the typical mutual fund. It has a large number of individual holdings —stocks or bonds or both— and can own tens of millions in capital in each of several of those holdings. It also holds some cash, in anticipation of acquiring more securities or of handling external cash flow. It is nearly always in the process of sending cash to some of its investors who redeem shares for their distribution needs. The manager does not hold too much cash, as it has little or no return—particularly in today's money markets—and he is judged upon the fund's total return. Cash doesn't help that judgment call.

When a market liquidity event occurs, there is always some running for the exits by investors. This drains the fund manager's cash position. If the drain becomes excessive, he will have to begin selling some of the fund's portfolio into a declining market. This selling, if reflective of other fund managers' activities, can exacerbate the decline and exaggerate the internal liquidity event. If leverage has been an aspect of the fund managers' approach, this worsens a bad situation. If the manager has positions in a market with a low liquidity horizon, the complexity can overwhelm his choice patterns. One has only to review Long-Term Capital Management, L.P. and the events of the late summer of 1997 to discover the result.

Sector rotation can also lead to internal liquidity issues for a fund if enough investors leave large cap growth and migrate to value. When the markets seize up, as recent events of 2008-2009 demonstrated, the cascade effect becomes ubiquitous—and disastrous. The fund manager has the Hobson's choice between holding to his investment objective (and bonus) and investor flight forcing him to sell to meet cash call. He will live to tell the tale. Will you? Markets can be irrational far longer than your personal liquidity horizon.

Fund performance issues result from investors chasing the best mutual funds in the market. Although we say it daily—"past performance is no indication of future results"—few listen; fewer still hear. Chasing performance appears to be actively encouraged in most of the advertising from fund companies. It is the mantra. It is a lie. It results in capital flows at the worst possible time to fund managers who are overwhelmed with new buys in a market that quickly becomes self-driven by their purchase orders. The market breaks down, the fund's performance drops. Capital flows outward to the next fund beastie. We want to be winners. We have short-term bias to the successful among us. We play the odds, as they are described to us by the industry.

Structural risk results from the nature of the design of a mutual fund. It is composed of at least a few dozen and as many as several hundred individual securities. In the case of bond funds, the design characteristic—many individual bonds—is meant to diversify across a section of the marketplace, to reduce the risk of exposure to any individual bond. The Law of Unintended Consequences—a corollary to Murphy's Law—creates a new type of risk.

You are fully vulnerable to the risk of rising interest rates, oncoming inflation, and lack of responsiveness to such changes. The fund values react directly and daily to perceived as well as real risk in these areas. With an individual bond held to maturity, the changes in its value each day are insignificant—and immaterial to your portfolio. Yes, it will still change as interest rates or inflation rise. The change will be far less than a mutual fund invested in the same market experiences. Because you will hold the bond to maturity, the yield to you will always and only be a function of the price you originally paid for the bond. When it matures, you get your capital back. Simple.

This is far simpler than the complex change in value of a mutual fund, particularly one invested in the bond markets. The price of the fund depends upon a host of factors outside of your venue.

All of the above referenced costs affect the price of the bond fund shares. The exogenous risks of the bond market add further price components to your bond mutual fund. The risk premium that you are willing to pay is far in excess of the result you will normally achieve.

You will earn the average yield of all of the bonds in the fund's portfolio. This yield will almost always be less than you can earn with a small group of well-chosen bonds. It will rapidly decline as investors pour into the fund in response to its latest advertising campaign—and as you reinvest each month's coupon at a lower yield and higher share price. As interest rates and inflation rise, you can expect a rapid response in the bond fund share price—downward. You can also expect the same with even the perception of an increase in interest rates or inflation. The recovery of share price from these declines often takes far longer than the precipitous drop.

Redemption costs can have a deleterious impact on your bond fund share price and/or yield. Most fund managers wisely keep 95% to 98% or more of their assets fully invested at all times. If inflation or interest rate scares rise up in the media, many foolish, fearful investors will sell their bond fund shares in panic. The fund manager must meet the redemption requests from all shareholders in a timely manner. He must raise cash to meet extraordinary redemptions. Once he burns through the 2% to

5% of the fund that he may hold in cash, he will have to begin selling bonds to meet the cash call. The order in which he meets this prescribed sell-off and the volume of sales the call demands will dictate the resulting yield and price to the remaining shareholders. If force of circumstance requires, he may have to dig deeply into the fund's portfolio to pay off the retreating shareholders. While this cascading effect often loses steam in a few days or weeks, the fiscal trauma to the remaining owners of the fund's shares can last for months. Tax consequences are shared at the end of the year. These final unpleasant surprises remove all doubt about the wisdom of having your entire bond portfolio held in bond mutual fund shares.

Why would you pay the average cost today's bond mutual fund ownership: more than .9%? What do you receive in exchange for this expense? You do not have to do the work. You can ignore the changes in the fixed income marketplace. You accept potentially lower returns. You participate in potentially higher volatility, in a lower volatility market. You pay taxes for redemptions you did not incur. You lose asset value for real and for perceived risk.

Congratulations.

The High Cost of Convenience

Investors believe that mutual funds offer the convenience of owning a wide spectrum of assets with a minimum of hassle. But that convenience comes at a price. The fees charged by a mutual fund and the costs associated with its ownership are a constant drain upon performance of even the best managed funds. They are also a constant source of discussion. Recently, kaChing held off against the Investment Company Institute (ICI) in a debate over actual expenses incurred by the average mutual fund investor: kaChing argued that 3.37% is the fee the average stock mutual fund investor pays, while ICI held to 1.17%. The analysts at kaChing took into account the taxable cost of transactions, which erode value even more so than fees. Those at ICI maintained the fund families' script. The debate will continue to rage, as each side has a vested interest and objectivity is lost in the discussion.

> **Fees charged by a mutual fund and the costs associated with its ownership are a constant drain upon performance of even the best managed funds.**

John Bogle—the founder of The Vanguard Group, its former CEO and a constant thorn in the side of the mutual fund industry—has made it quite clear. Fund expenses do no shareholder good—except those who are the managers of the funds. He quotes a recent study by Morningstar indicating that "using fund-expenses ratios as a factor in choosing mutual funds was even more helpful than relying upon its (Morningstar's) own carefully constructed star ratings." Specifically, focusing on funds with the lowest expense ratios was more helpful in 58% of the time periods studied. In every asset class (US stock funds, international stock funds, balanced funds, taxable bond funds, and municipal bond funds) over every time period, "the cheapest quintile produced higher net returns than the most expensive quintile."

Over a 50-year investing time horizon, the difference in return for a low cost domestic equity fund versus a higher cost fund—1.3%—would create 50% more capital to the shareholder! Irrespective of the huge increase in the size of the industry (from $500 billion in 1960 to $5 trillion in 2010), economies of scale do not transfer down to the shareholder. Fees have increased over that same time span. Expense ratios have declined. Average expense ratios are .84% today, down from .86% in 2000 and up from .54% in 1960. Returns have been hit deeper and deeper.

For the dividend seeker, mutual funds are a cancer upon your portfolio. These dividends and their reinvestment make up more than 80% of the return in the S&P 500 index. Fund expenses consumed nearly 20% of the average equity fund income in 1960. In 2009, they consumed nearly 40% of that same dividend income. Thus, that ratty little average equity fund yielded less than 1% in 2009.

Buyer, Be Aware

If you use mutual funds, be aware of the costs. You are paying for investment advice. It is rarely delivered consistently. It is exceedingly rarely delivered in excess of what you potentially can receive from a passive index investment approach. No fund or manager can beat the market for long. Accept that as demonstrable. Institutional players, such as large mutual fund managers, are the market. They provide the liquidity and demand. Their flows can drive prices and markets far longer than is warranted by the value of the securities in those markets. This distorts the landscape.

Today, the newest challenge is from high speed traders. They typically account for 60% to 70% of daily volume on the NYSE and NASDAQ. They place huge bets on penny changes in the price of stocks and indices. They do so with lightning speed. They can get in and out in milliseconds. They step in between trades and execute both sides of a trade and no one knows the better. The "mini crash" of May 2010 was probably a direct result of their behavior. They trade for profit. In so doing, they are the ultimate market makers. They are also the ultimate market destroyers. Their heightened velocity and high volume trades can have a devastating impact on prices and availability to smaller investors. Until their behavior is modified or controlled or eliminated, no value investor is safe from their potential impact.

Imagine a small river flowing through fields. Farmers on either side may divert some of the water for their crops. Their diversion does not materially affect the river flow. Imagine now the river swelling with spring floods. The banks overflow, the fields are awash. The excess of water overpowers the fields. For a time, the alluvial deposits may provide sustenance. If the river does not fall back to its lower level, the fields are drowned. The crops are destroyed.

So, too, can markets be affected by a constant supply of capital. An occasional excess may be beneficial. A torrent of capital will eventually drown the markets, drive prices beyond reason and destroy value. The result may be a depletion of wealth.

Thus, you are paying for something other than performance. If you are paying an investment professional to pay attention while you do something else, fine. If you are paying them because you have no interest in the subject, okay. If you are paying them because your friend does or because you heard it through the grapevine, then you are the greater fool. Your money will be soon parted from you—or worse, parted from you over many years as a Chinese water torture trick.

In Hemingway's *The Sun Also Rises* his character, Mike, is asked how he went bankrupt. His answer might apply here: "Two ways," Mike said. "Gradually and then suddenly."

ELECTRONICALLY TRADED FUNDS (ETFs)

An electronically traded fund (ETF) is a security that operates as an index fund—around a group of similar assets—but trades like a stock on an exchange.[2]

ETFs have several distinct features:

- They trade during market session.
- They are transparent—you know what you get.
- Their fees are significantly lower than mutual fund fees.
- They may trade at or below par, infrequently.
- Their daily volumes can affect their price.
- They are designed for and used by institutional investors.

There are many bond ETFs available today, with others planned. These can be excellent alternatives to bond funds and even to individual bond portfolios. The pricing and yields are quite competitive.[3]

As we discussed in the chapter on bonds, pricing can be a challenge. If you are not careful, you will pay as much or more than you would with the average bond mutual fund. Recall that you pay when you buy and again if you need to sell. The spread you are charged can have a deleterious impact upon your cost and your yield. Be aware of costs.

CLOSED END FUNDS (CEFS)

Closed end funds (CEFs) are similar to mutual funds, with the major difference being they have a fixed number of securities within their structure. Closed end funds are far more transparent—you know what is inside. Shares are traded between market participants, rather than from fund to shareholder, as with a mutual fund.

The price of the CEF fluctuates with the perception of the value of the stocks or bonds inside. Their prices can trade above or below par—that is, the actual value of the basket of securities they hold. Price may be based upon other characteristics: market liquidity, liquidity of the held securities, amount of cash held, and unrealized gains or losses.

The liquidity horizon of CEFs can expand and contract with demand. Thus, the shares trade at a premium or a discount to the value of the underlying securities. Buying at a discount may make sense, if you know why the discount is priced into the fund. Many do use leverage to enhance yield; you should know how much.

You do want to read the prospectus for any CEF you are considering. It lists the securities, payout rates and dates, amount of leverage available for use, etc.

The first observation may be the dividend. You want to know more than the yield, however. How was the yield justified? Is it dividend, gains, or both? Is it equalized over the year? Is it because of significant leverage? What is the amount of undistributed net investment income (UNII)? Is the yield a partial return of principal? Is it in excess of comparable unit investment trusts (UITs)? If it trades at a premium to others of similar nature, be wary. Why does it command a higher price?

There are nearly 600 closed end funds currently in the US. Your information sources should include but not be limited to:

- Closed-endfunds.com: the CEFA website; a great education with information updated daily
- Quantumonline.com: an excellent source for CEFs, UITs, MLPs, REITs, preferreds, and other yield based investments
- Dividendinvestor.com: an excellent comparison viewing tool
- FINVIZ.com: the site for complex information
- NYSE.com: all stock information
- NASDAQ.com: exchanges

As of 12/31/10, a review of cefa.com showed that of the 127 equity CEFs, 100 have yields over 6%. Of the 407 debt CEFs, 276 have yields over 6%. Of the 63 foreign CEFs, 23 have yields over the 6% benchmark.

Closed end funds may play only a small part in your portfolio. They have a complexity all their own that requires knowledge and skill. Many investors will shy away from complex instruments with sometimes limited liquidity. The severe downdrafts that can occur here are not for the timid.

The leverage play of many CEFs runs contrary to our quest for low debt investments. It is further complicated by the UNII issue. Debt always brings more to the table than simply enhanced return to the investor. It brings risk and volatility; again, we are trying to avoid these traps.

The callable features can leave you with cash when you want yield. You have to go shopping again for a new yield play. Most CEFs are issued by banks. You would like to find non-bank CEFs, such as those issued by manufacturing firms or utilities.

It is a sector of the marketplace that may be visited upon occasion, upon a rapid fall in pricing, for example. You must do your homework at sites like quantumonline.com. Do not enter this field unprepared or you will leave it stripped of good sense.

WORKSHEET

Assignment: Explore helpful websites.

Visit the following websites. Spend as much time as you can at each site, learning, discovering, and experimenting. Subscribe to the site if it interests you.

Ici.org (another point of view on fund fees!)
Quantumonline.com
Preferreds.com
Dividenddetective.com
Cefa.com
Preferredstockinvesting.com

8

THE CASE FOR ANNUITIES

"The man who makes everything
that leads to happiness depend upon himself,
and not upon other men, has adopted
the very best plan for living happily."
—Plato

hen selecting income generating investments for your retirement portfolio, a private annuity from an insurance company can be a beneficial addition because it provides:

+ an income stream you cannot outlive
+ the psychological security of a known income each month
+ a simple risk management tool

What Is an Annuity?

An annuity is a financial product that is designed to pay out a steady stream of income over time. For example, your retirement benefit from the Social Security Administration is an annuity: an income stream you cannot outlive whose value is defined by your tenure in the workplace and your earnings during that time. If you have a pension from a private company or from a public entity—a school district, peace officers association, hospital, government entity, or the like—then you have an annuity. The pension administrator will be sending you a sum each month whose value is based upon your tenure and your income. Annuities also are offered and guaranteed by insurance companies. These benefits are guaranteed by the claims paying ability and financial stability of the issuing insurance company.

> **The psychological advantages to a guaranteed income stream that you cannot outlive are enormous.**

Called private annuities or personal annuities, they are purchased for a sum of capital paid in over a period of time or in a lump sum.

The psychological advantages to a guaranteed income stream that you cannot outlive are enormous. If you have a guarantee of income from Social Security, you feel better about your retirement. If you have a similar guarantee from your state pension or your employer, your positive attitude toward a comfortable retirement increases substantially. The original premise for Social Security was to act as the third leg of the retirement stool: work pension, personal savings, and Supplemental Security Income (SSI). It promised a secure income during the last years of citizenship. Such a promise was itself based upon the annuity concept from the life insurance industry.

Unfortunately, today Social Security is publicly funded with current tax cash flow. There are no amounts set aside—they have already been spent by a profligate politic. The promise to you is an unfunded liability of the US government. Whether it will be there for you during retirement may be a political question.

Annuities: A Time Honored Investment

The history of annuities begins in Rome, where you could make a payment to the *annua* in exchange for an annual income payment during your life. The tontine was used by European governments during the late Middle Ages to fund their interminable wars against one another or to support or defy a religious order. A contribution would guarantee an income stream to the nominee for life, gradually growing for the survivors as each nominee died.

In the English Colonies in 1759, the Commonwealth of Pennsylvania allowed a company to form for the benefit of Presbyterian ministers. People would contribute to the annuity in exchange for lifetime income. During the US Depression, life insurance companies were viewed as stable institutions in a world gone awry. Their popularity spread as annuity firms were increasingly seen as a safe alternative to the vicissitudes of the markets and the conniving of "stock jobbers."

The saving habits of a nation were ideally suited for the long-term time horizon of the insurance company. These companies were, and are, very secure in their ability to match their portfolios to their obligations. Income was guaranteed for a set amount or a set period, with the interest rate set and guaranteed as well.

Social Security itself was based upon the concept of a forced savings plan coupled with a guaranteed income for life. Its original premise—the assumed short lifespan of the typical retiree in the mid-20th century—has been proven false. We live longer and healthier lives today than our forebears lived. Consequently, the income stream needed to support us has lengthened considerably. There are more of us retirees today, growing by three to four million each year.[1] We're supported by fewer workers, who are earning more and expecting their own retirement benefits. The formula for SSI is a complex social and political issue. Whether Social

Security remains a stable source of income for Baby Boomers or whether it is resting upon a sea of mud remains to be seen.

Types of Annuities

Much thought and design have gone into the new generation of annuities. In exchange for an amount of capital, today's life insurers will guarantee an income stream for a period of time. That guarantee is often well purchased. Insurance company annuities typically come in four varieties: immediate, fixed, variable, and index. We'll discuss each of these below.

Immediate Annuities. An immediate annuity makes payments immediately or soon after purchase. This type of annuity can be the simplest means to reaching your income goal upon retirement. Once you have identified your retirement income sources and amounts, you will have a sense of what you will need to meet your income goal. You can purchase an immediate annuity that covers your monthly fixed income need for your life and for that of your spouse. Each insurance company will pay a slightly different amount, based upon the sum you invest with it, the life expectancies the carrier builds into its assumptions, and the current interest rate. Inflation adjustments will need to be met elsewhere.

With an immediate annuity you choose to annuitize a certain amount of capital. That means you accept a set amount of income for an agreed-upon period of time. You give the insurance carrier an amount of capital and they give you monthly or quarterly income for the time guaranteed. The amount you receive is both interest and principal, the mix a function of your age and the type of settlement. The interest is taxable; the principal is free of taxation.

Immediate annuities come in two varieties: fixed and variable. A fixed settlement is as stated above. A variable settlement amount is dependent upon the performance of an underlying basket of securities. The variable settlement can be a minimum fixed amount plus the variable amount or purely the variable amount. The variable amount usually updates once a year. You might choose a variable settlement as a way to approach inflation. As inflation rises, so too might the value of the underlying portfolio, thus enhancing the chance for you to increase your income next year.

Fixed Annuities. The simplest annuity is the fixed annuity.[2] It offers a guaranteed interest rate for a period of time, typically from six months to ten years. The rate can change only when the time period is complete. The new rate offered may or may not be similar to current time deposit rates. The insurer is the guarantor of the principal and interest.

The advantage of a fixed rate annuity is that you are guaranteed the fixed rate, regardless of the performance of the underlying investments. The disadvantage is that these annuities offer limited room for growth. Even if the underlying investments perform spectacularly, you will still receive the fixed amount.

Variable Annuities. A more complex form of annuity is the variable annuity.[3] Variable annuities do just that—their value varies with the underlying asset mix that you choose. You give the insurance firm a set amount of capital—or invest a regular amount over a period of time—and you have a choice of investments within the contract. The choices may be limited or there may be several dozen subaccounts from which to choose. These are often mutual funds held within the annuity, much like the funds you know. You can invest according to an allocation strategy or according to your best judgment.

When you are ready to receive income from the annuity contract, you can take out a certain amount monthly, at your discretion, or you can annuitize. Annuitize means that you give the insurance company the funds, irrevocably. In exchange they give you a monthly income. If you annuitize, then the monthly income can be fixed or variable, as you choose.

Variable annuities now come in an amazing complexity of choices. These alternatives are priced to you for a fee, usually a percent of the account value. You may decide that you want to have a guaranteed lifetime benefit, for example. This assures you that when you take income, you will receive a set percentage of the account value for your life or the lives of you and your spouse. These contract riders are called guaranteed minimum withdrawal benefits (GMWBs). Their calculation could be the subject for an entire book and is embedded in the prospectus you receive with the investment. Riders are additional guarantee options that are available to annuity or life insurance contract holders. While some riders are part of an existing contract, others may carry additional fees, charges, and restrictions. You should review the contract carefully before purchasing.

You need a good agent, financial advisor, or website comparison tool to ascertain the differences between the GMWBs and any other available riders from various carriers. You should expect an objective comparison from your advisor, clearly delineating the differences, the advantages, and the disadvantages of each. Understand that once you invest in a variable annuity with a GMWB, you have made a lifetime decision. Make it with care and with consideration. **Ignore** any sales pitch: "Have we got a deal for you!"

You can also purchase a guaranteed minimum account value rider. This assures the account will grow by a certain percentage each year, or the actual growth of the subaccount(s), whichever is greater. You can buy riders that offer enhanced death benefits for your heirs. For example, you can buy a rider to pay a portion of estimated estate taxes. Each of these riders will have a price attached, clearly stated. In many cases, the benefit may be well worth the cost.

Index Annuities. Index annuities are the most complex forms of the annuity vehicle. Their value is based upon the change in an underlying index over a given period of time. The change may have a guaranteed floor. For example, with a 2% guaranteed floor, the account will grow by at least this amount each year. The manner in which the value is tied to the index, the index itself, how the difference is computed, and how often this occurs are all aspects of the decision making process. These decisions have to be made before the purchase, as they are set thereafter. You might consider an index annuity if you do not want the responsibility of investment decision making but desire the potential of returns greater than those offered in the fixed annuity field.

Equity indexed annuities (EIAs) are not suitable for all investors. EIAs permit investors to participate in only a stated percentage of an increase in an index (participation rate) and may impose a maximum annual account value percentage increase. EIAs typically do not allow for participation in dividends accumulated on the securities represented by the index. EIAs are long-term, tax-deferred investment vehicles designed for retirement purposes. Withdrawals prior to 59-1/2 may result in a 10% IRS penalty tax and surrender charges may apply. As with other types of annuities, the guarantees are based on the claims paying ability of the issuer.

The Best Annuity for You

Finding the right annuity will require some legwork but once selected, can serve you well. There are many variants within each type of annuity and as stated above, you can purchase riders to ensure a variety of outcomes. For example, you may wish to ensure income for you, or for you and your heir. You may want to ensure a certain basic rate of return. You may wish to choose the underlying investments themselves, for which you will pay a management fee. You can take risk or avoid risk. You can buy a guaranteed income for a period of time: your life, a certain number of years, or a combination of both.

If simple solutions are what you seek, then fixed or immediate annuities probably make sense. If you are able to take some risk but do not want to be too involved with the details, then a variable annuity with an asset allocation strategy within its subaccounts may make sense. If you choose this option, you should be comfortable re-allocating your portfolio from time to time or using an internal program to do so for you.

Suppose you are looking for a guaranteed income stream. You do not want to think about markets, investments, the economy, or stop losses. How do you use an annuity? You know when you want to receive the monthly income: now (immediate annuity) or later (fixed or variable).

An immediate annuity strategy should use a multi-year laddering strategy. For example, you may have a series of bank CDs with maturities spread out over five years. At each maturity you might acquire an immediate annuity. If interest rates rise during these five years, then each annuity you purchase will have a slightly higher monthly distribution amount. If interest rates decline over the five years, then you will have the highest distribution amount coming to you for a longer time, because you purchased it first, when rates were higher.

A fixed annuity strategy means you are willing to wait for some years before taking monthly income from your annuities. Again, you would purchase the series over a period of years, laddering as before. We ladder because we have no idea what interest rates will do, so choose to participate in them over a time series. We are attempting to manage duration risk.

A variable annuity strategy is more complex. First, you do not need the income now. Second, you are comfortable managing a portfolio. Third, you are not that comfortable doing so. Fourth, you are willing to buy the guarantee. Fifth, you do not want to put all your assets into one basket. Finally, you have some idea of how much you need and when. With these criteria in mind, you can use a variable annuity. It covers all these bases. You can defer receiving a portion of your retirement income until a later date while managing the portfolio, all the while having a floor to support your portfolio risk, one for which you are willing to pay the price.

Keep in mind that each annuity contract will contain its own expenses. Any laddering strategy should include a comprehensive evaluation of the fees associated with the strategy prior to implementation.

Buying Annuities for the Long Term

If you find that you do not need additional income in the year that you retire but will need it in the future, then an annuity may be of value, too. You may have an income from the sale of your business, from the sale of an asset, or from an inheritance. This income allows you to postpone drawing on your annuity. Typically, the longer you wait until you take withdrawal, the greater the value in investing in an annuity vehicle. As long-term investment vehicles, they are structured to accrue benefits to you over time. The longer the time, the greater the benefit. The process of deferred growth allows for greater wealth creation.

The use of a variable annuity with a guaranteed minimum withdrawal benefit (GMWB) ultimately allows you to manage the far horizon of longevity risk. You invest capital in this type of annuity, hold it for the very long term (20+ years), and turn to it for income during your eighties or nineties. You pay for the benefit of a withdrawal amount based upon a fixed percentage of a stepped-up value each year. This prevents the potential ravages of inflation from eroding your purchasing power by offering an ultimate income stream growing at a rate ideally keeping pace with inflation. You may choose to be more aggressive with this portfolio piece because of these annual "step ups" in value. When the portfolio rises significantly because of good market performance, the new contract value and its guaranteed income are based upon the new "highest daily value" or "highest quarterly value." The longer you live, the greater this benefit to you becomes.

What Do Annuities Cost?

Annuities do come with costs. You may earn better returns by owning individual securities. The fees for these variable annuities can be more than 4% a year, driving down potential account value increases. In the best of all possible worlds, you may receive as much as 5% a year in growth.

Then why invest in an annuity?

Because despite these costs, an annuity protects you from the risk of "sequence of returns"—the risk of receiving lower or negative returns—which you may see in your portfolio despite the best intentions of your stop loss program. By placing some of your assets with an insurance company and receiving an annuity, you reduce the possibility that a significant market downturn will impact your lifestyle. No matter what happens in the marketplace, your annuity payment remains the same, thus removing you from marketplace risk.

Annuity costs can be complex and hidden. Recall that the insurance carrier assures you of a monthly income stream for a period of time. The amount is determined by the capital invested, the time period, the carrier's investment experience, and the expected profitability on the contract. The carrier will offer you an illustration of the various settlement options. Few will tell you the interest rate they apply to the settlement, but you can figure that rate out easily enough. It can be as high as 3% from a good carrier to less than 1% from a profit seeking company. Be aware. Do the math first.

Immediate annuity costs are hidden within the investment. They are obvious, however, from the monthly income you will receive. The better the income stream, the lower the expense, all else being equal. Also, the more experienced insurance firms will have greater skill in matching liabilities to capital. This will be reflected in their distribution to you. Better paying insurance companies can offer significantly more per month based on the same $100,000 invested, so it's wise to shop around. You can easily shop on the internet for immediate annuities offering a variety of rates.

Fixed annuity costs typically only involve a surrender charge. This is a fee the carrier takes from the account value if you leave before a specified period of time. It can be anywhere from one year to infinity. They may charge an MVA—market value adjustment—if you take from the account more than the 10% each year that you are usually allowed.

Variable annuity costs may include a number of fees and charges, the most common of which are listed below.

- *Mortality and expense charge*: the cost to insure the principal at risk as the carrier sees it.

- *Administration fee*: usually $30 annually for smaller accounts (less than $100,000).
- *Distribution fee*: the fee the carrier pays an advisor to sell you the product.
- *Investment fees*: the mutual fund companies' fees.
- *Switching fees*: fees assessed if you move within variable subaccounts more often that 24 to 30 times each year.
- *MVA (market value adjustment)*: the cost that may be assessed if you move out of a fixed investment portfolio within the time period.
- *Surrender charge*: the cost that may be assessed if you sell or withdraw during the surrender period, typically six to eight years from the time of purchase.

Index annuity costs can be the most complex in structure. You need to know which index the carrier uses, how it determines the change in value of that index, and how you participate in that change. It can be a simple annual change in value, a point-to-point change, or a quarterly change, to name but a few. Your participation rate may be 100%, 110%, 90%, or 100% up to a certain ceiling (say 8%). It can be adjusted over more or less than one year. It may have lifetime rate caps as well.

The most callous use of fees is the two tiered annuity structure. Here, you can "enjoy" the participation rate of the carrier's choice. The first tier applies if you surrender the annuity before hell freezes over and take your money elsewhere; your account value is usually assessed a surrender charge that can be as high as 15% of your invested capital. The account will actually have grown by only a small annual interest rate, less than the guaranteed 2%. It will not have "participated" in any index over any time. The carrier wants your money and good luck getting it back. You have to annuitize to get any real value. The second tier is the annuitization. Your capital is often annuitized at a rate of 1% or less. The motive is profit seeking, at your expense.

The acid test of any annuity is the commission. What does the life agent earn as a commission on the amount of the sale of the product to you? Ask him. Most fixed and immediate annuities pay a commission of 1% to 2%; most variable annuities pay 1% to 6%, plus an annual "trail" of .15% to 1.25%. Some index annuities pay as much as 10% to the agent up front. The agent can also earn other perks, such as free trip rewards. The more the insurance company pays in commission to the agent, the more they have to charge you to recoup their up-front cost. They will charge, so ask.

If the agent earns an annual fee based upon how well your accounts perform, he is at least tied to you at the waist. His income grows with the success of your portfolio and declines when the accounts decline. He should be more attentive here. This is the least you can expect of his time and knowledge.

You do not have to buy an annuity from an agent. You can buy them direct and you can buy them without a surrender charge and with significantly lower fees. Vanguard, Fidelity, and T. Rowe Price are examples of low cost fixed or variable annuity providers. The flat fee annuity is another choice for many. You pay only the subaccount fee, switching fees, plus a fee assigned by your advisor. Again, she is compensated based upon the value of your account. Its decline reduces her income; its increase gives her valuable recompense. Expect that, at least.

Time and the Annuity

According to current actuarial tables, a healthy 65-year-old couple has a greater than 50% chance that at least one partner will live beyond 90. An annuity is simply the transfer of this longevity risk to an insurance company for a fee. Whether it is an immediate annuity, a fixed annuity or a variable one, your task is to ensure that what you are paying for offers the risk transfer you seek.

In exchange for this fee, you will not outlive your money. It is really quite simple. You buy peace of mind. You acquire the same type of security you seek with auto, homeowner, personal or business liability, disability and life insurance premium payments. The size of the premium, the costs inherent in the contract, and the quality of the underwriting insurance firm are all yours to determine. As you shop for auto insurance, so you shop for retirement income insurance.

Time is your greatest ally when you make an annuity purchase. Your age, health, and time horizon for needing income are among your most important considerations when viewing an annuity investment. A long, healthy life under a low tax regime can make the right annuity a fine asset. Work with an insurance company with these assumptions in mind.

Many annuities today offer a guaranteed doubling of value each ten years. The Rule of 72 states that if you divide the rate of return by 72, you determine how many years it will take to double the account value. Thus, doubling your capital in ten years requires an annual return of 7.18%. Interesting how close this is to our 7%![4]

The longer you have until you need the income from the annuity, the better positioned it can be to potentially grow the capital base—the base which will provide you with the income you need. Tax deferral is the reason. The earnings of an annuity contract develop each year without taxation. Positive earnings lead to further growth upon a larger capital base.

Understand that the growth in a variable annuity may be a result of capital gains, interest, or dividends. All earnings distributions from annuities are taxed as ordinary income. In exchange for long-term tax deferral, you give up annual taxation or capital gains and dividends at capital gains rates. Currently these tax rates are lower than ordinary income. This is neither a positive nor a negative outcome. It is a point of awareness for the knowledgeable investor.

The longer you may expect to live also works to your advantage in considering an annuity. A payment for twenty years is more valuable than that same amount for fifteen years; one for forty years is more valuable than one for twenty. If you and your family live long, healthy existences, then a guaranteed lifetime income stream is quite valuable.

The Effects of Taxes and Inflation on Annuities

Taxes due are deferred on annuities until you begin to withdraw payments. When you receive income from an annuity, it is taxed as ordinary income, just like a distribution from a retirement plan. The income you take is taxed as interest first, then return of principal, which is tax free. Immediate annuities give their monthly income as both taxed and tax free income.

Thus, your second challenge when considering an annuity is the tax rate you will face upon distribution from the account. Taxes can either remain at their current levels, decrease, or increase. The first has never happened; each year taxes change at virtually every level of governmental interference in your personal income. You may be quite good at avoiding taxation because of good tax counsel, but the changes happen regardless.

Will taxes decline? Your answer should certainly be weighted to the negative. Many Baby Boomers agree that the nation and their communities simply have too much current debt and deferred obligations to seriously consider reducing taxation in our lifetimes. An explosive growth in the economy engendered by significant changes to the Tax Code—perhaps simplification to a minimum of brackets and deductions—could lead to such wealth creation, subject to taxation, that the $14 trillion in national debt will shrink. *Inshallah,* as our Islamic friends would say.

You face, at best, a 50/50 chance of taxes increasing during your retirement. If they do, then the deferral of taxes until a later date can be advantageous. This can be advantageous because each year's legal non-payment of taxes accrues the taxed amount to your account. This is the way funds accumulating within your retirement account work. No withdrawals allow for greater accumulation. Certainly, if tax rates are higher when you take the income from the annuity, your net will be reduced. You can speculate as to what tax rate will have the most deleterious effect upon your distribution schedule. Given that this is pure speculation—we cannot know the future—the exercise may lead more to a futile expectation than to a safe prediction. Some calculations are indeed impossible.

What of inflation risk with an annuity? Recall our choice of approach with bonds—we laddered duration to affect better yield and avoid capital risk. The same idea applies to annuities. You can ladder them by purchasing them each year and acquiring differing yields from the fixed or immediate type. In a $1 million portfolio, you might place $400,000 in four fixed or immediate annuities over four years. Ideally, these will offer a stream of income that is different for each contract, growing as inflation rises.

Researching Annuities for Your Portfolio

A significant amount of academic work has been written on the subject of annuities. While simple in concept, annuities are quite complex in their detail. You'll want to research with care, or engage an independent advisor who can do so.

Your work begins with a reading of a few firm's prospectuses of their annuity products. While daunting, these are approachable. They are written by the marketing department, the compliance area, and the legal department. Expect obfuscation. Review from the index, first looking for topics of immediate interest: product description, risk factors, and costs. Then review the internal investments, the subaccounts. While of ultimate interest to you, understanding these is less important than understanding how the annuity will pay you the ultimate income stream that you are purchasing. Jump around to seek answers to your questions. Ignore the legalese during your first read. Come back to it once you have an understanding of the basic features of the product. Develop a list of questions to ask your advisor or to direct to the insurance company. They will be very pleased to answer these questions! Do not be put off by the format. Plow through, ask questions, make informed decisions. When you invest capital with a life insurance company, it is for the long haul. Walk in with your eyes open and you won't be disappointed later.

The quality of the insurance company to which you give your capital is of great importance, certainly. There are hundreds of companies. They are rated by a variety of agencies: Fitch, S&P, A.M. Best, and Moody's. Each evaluates criteria they judge most important and each takes a slightly different approach. A superior rating from at least three of the four should assure you of the carrier's standing.

It is rare that a carrier will suffer from financial difficulties sufficient to warrant concern, but from time to time they have problems. The state in which each company is domiciled has a fund that adds a further layer of protection. In the event that the carrier is unable to pay claims, the state fund is drawn upon to aid claimants. This world of insurance is quite different from that of most investment companies. Insurers tend to look out for one another, as sharks do. If one fails, it reflects poorly upon the others. Historically, failed firms have quickly been acquired by stronger companies and all claims paid. The weak are consumed by the strong.

The point of our discussion on costs and research is not to scare you away from the annuity idea or its purchase. It is to help you make an informed decision. The decision should not be solely based upon cost. Nor should it be solely based upon the creditworthiness of the insurance company. It should be based upon a variety of criteria:

- Your income need
- Your age (and perhaps that of your spouse)
- Your current tax situation
- Your risk tolerance
- Your attitude towards investing and saving
- Your timeline
- Continuity of the insurance company
- Costs
- Type of contract

For those of you in need of a deeper understanding of the annuity world, your journey will take you further afield. For an academic's approach to the issue of annuities, you should review the work of Dr. Moshe Milevsky of York University in Toronto. A long-time critic of annuities, he has recently come around to a more supportive attitude toward their wise use. He now makes the case for the use of annuities to manage longevity risk, inflation, and his self-defined "sequence of returns" risk. His new book, *Pensionize Your Nest Egg*, describes the challenges and opportunities of using annuities for retirement. *Are You a Stock or a Bond?*

also addresses the personal aspect of saving for and enjoying retirement. Dr. Milevsky has written for many years on the subject. His analysis may be controversial at times, but it is thorough.

The Role of the Annuity in Your 7% Portfolio

Ultimately, the annuity represents the first tier of your retirement income. Your company pension is the second tier, if you have one. The third tier, if applicable, belongs to the underfunded liability represented by the government pension from your state. The unfunded liability of Social Security is the fourth tier. Fifth, you have your personal retirement account, your IRA or 401(k) funds. Sixth is the icing for your cake: your personal assets. These could be a portfolio of stocks and bonds. They could be your business, its sales proceeds, your rental property, or a charitable remainder trust. Finally, you have your labor to fall back upon—you can work, or go back to work, if you choose.

These rankings, significantly different from what you have read from other sources, are ranked in terms of funded liability and of risk. You will know the risk of your real estate (occupancy levels, leverage, and property quality) and of your portfolio. You should be realistic about the risk of relying upon a government for your retirement security. If you assume those funds may not be there, then you can be more truthful with yourself about the risks of the remainder of the portfolio.

This risk analysis may lead you to the realization that private annuities from life insurance companies are well worth the price you pay. In exchange for a steep fee of as much as 3% or more each year, you will have the assurance of an income stream fully supported by a profitable company with its own and your interests in mind.

WORKSHEET

Assignment: Read detailed annuity storylines such as:

Moshe Milevsky, *Are You a Stock or a Bond?*, Chapters 9 - 10 (Upper Saddle River, NJ: FT Press, 2008).

Olivia Mitchell, Pension Research Council, "Securing Lifetime Retirement Income." Excerpt available with synopsis at pensionresearchcouncil.org.

You need to know more than a prospectus will tell you. These two voices are from academia, so the reading is advanced, but well worthwhile.

UNUSUAL INCOME SOURCES: MLPS AND BDCS

"Take calculated risks. That is quite different from being rash."
—General George S. Patton

The income sources for you in retirement extend beyond stocks, bonds, bank CDs, money markets, funds, and annuities. In this chapter we'll explore master limited partnerships—MLPs (including their close cousins, LLCs) and business development corporations—BDCs. While tax forms sometimes refer to them as "unusual income sources," they can, when prudently selected, provide a major boost to your portfolio's income. But before you invest, it's imperative that you understand how these investments work—their risks and their rewards.

MASTER LIMITED PARTNERSHIPS AND LLCS

Master limited partnerships—MLPs—are companies that are organized as limited partnerships and whose units trade on a securities exchange. The technical term is PTP: publicly traded partnerships. This class of equities also includes limited liability companies—LLCs. They have both general partners, who manage the firms, and limited partners, who are passive investors. They offer significant income, a fairly well non-correlated asset class (think diversification), and real tax advantages. In exchange for these benefits, you accept the risks associated with infrastructure investment, the challenges of midcap, small, and microcap markets, the volatility that comes with issues trading at lower volumes, tax complexity, energy prices, international events, and potential interest rate sensitivity.

Most MLPs invest in energy infrastructure. The vast majority are owners of energy extractors, pipelines, distribution centers, terminals, transportation, and tank farms. A few others—some grandfathered into the MLP world—invest in real estate, private equity, funds, timberland, amusement parks, fertilizer products, and even cemeteries. The National Association of Publicly Traded Partnerships includes both MLPs and others without the MLP structure. There are as of this writing more than 100 publicly traded partnerships (PTPs) listed on the association's website.

What MLPs Offer and How They Work

MLPs typically offer a high degree of current income, as they own assets which generate significant free cash flow each year. These assets are usually mineral related (oil, natural gas, propane), which have high depreciation (and depletion) rates. The MLPs usually don't own the mineral; they simply receive a "toll" for the passage of the mineral down their specific toll way—pipeline, tanker, storage tank, or distribution center. The fee they receive is a function of the volume that passes through, the mineral type, the negotiated rate of passage, and the governmental (FERP) guidelines. It is important to understand how little relationship there is to the commodity price, how much to its demand. Oil, natural gas, propane, etc. have their own markets, values, pricing mechanisms, and cost features. MLPs and the fees they receive for the transportation of these commodities are only obliquely related to these markets. MLP share prices will react to events in these markets, but often only asymmetrically in time. That is, their price reaction to commodity prices will be temporary, a reflection of the market's "knee jerk reaction" to external stimuli.

The typical, mainstream commodity firm has spun off these mineral extraction, transportation, processing, and storage assets, as they are relatively low earnings producers as standalone entities. The price of the typical MLP has relatively low volatility in most markets. MLPs' dividend growth rate can be significant: the firms usually increase their payouts as their net income grows. An MLP's net income has a natural tendency to grow because of reasonably low overhead—along with the aforementioned depreciation—and incentive distribution rights (IDRs).

The general partners of most MLPs structure their compensation so that they receive more income as they pay out more net income to investors. This is a compensation scheme designed with the investor in mind—you have to like it. Unlike many other companies—which design compensation structures as incredibly complex tools to draw off income and assets from a firm to its senior management—MLPs compensate their senior management for paying more distributions to unit holders. Their very structure is intended to pay out at least 90% of income to unit holders.

Long-term debt is almost always lower than 50%. Their bond yields are lower than their dividends, fairly unusual in the stock market (and a ringer for most stocks, when this occurs). The implication is clear: the capital markets view the debt very favorably. There is significant capital capacity to service the debt. The chance that it will default is low and the markets price it accordingly.

The additional income from the MLP portion of your portfolio has the potential to increase the overall portfolio return significantly. If 10% of your securities are MLPs earning 10% and you have a $500,000 portfolio, then $50,000 is held in this asset and these investments would earn you $5,000. If they were held in an asset earning 5%, you would earn $2,500. That increase in earnings is one-half of 1% of the overall portfolio's yield. Put another way, you would need twice as much capital to earn the same amount: $100,000 at 5% earns you $5,000. Diversification by income source and type allows you to seek and earn higher income.

The History of MLPs

Apache Oil was the first MLP in 1981, followed rapidly by nearly 100 other corporate conversions and esoteric public offerings, including the Boston Celtics. The relevant and obvious tax abuses were addressed by the Tax Reform Act of 1986, followed by the Revenue Act of 1987. Both resulted in limiting the MLP structure to those companies where at least 90% of their income was "qualifying income"—"income and gains derived from the exploration, development, mining or production, processing, refining, transportation (including pipelines, transporting of gas, oil, or similar products), or the marketing of any mineral or natural resources including fertilizer, geothermal energy, and timber." The qualifying income is characterized as distributions rather than dividends. Of the original MLPs, only three remain today.

The MLP market quickly evolved to include oil and gas activities of exploration and production. The self-liquidating nature of the business—and the speculative nature of exploration—proved unable to support significant distributions. During the early 1990s, the energy giants began to unload their low growth assets. The transportation, refining, and storage parts of their business— the boring parts—were spun off to the MLP structure, as originally envisioned by the legislation. MLPs have been reborn today.

What to Look for in an MLP

If you are looking for one of the less aggressive (in other words, less risky) MLP firms, here are the characteristics you want to see:

+ Low commodity price exposure
+ Fee based revenue streams contracted out several years
+ Low leverage reflected in distribution coverage ratios
+ Capital markets access at reasonable prices
+ Acquisition strategies accretive to net income

If you are searching for a more aggressive MLP (in other words, higher yield), here are the characteristics you'll want to see:

+ Hedged commodity portfolio maintenance
+ Higher gearing ratios
+ Ability to respond to an economic recovery via turnover
+ Pending capital expenditure projects anticipating lower cost of capital
+ Financial discipline

Tax Advantages

Tax concerns are the first hurdle with MLPs. All tax results— both earnings and reporting requirements—are passed on to the limited partner or unit holder, thus avoiding the typical dual taxation of the C corporation. Distributions are based upon distributable cash flow. Institutional investors—mutual funds, pensions, and endowments—usually avoid this type of investment, because the market—in terms of both shares outstanding and typical volume—is too small for their needs and the tax consequences are too complicated for large scale asset managers. Endowments have specific tax reasons to avoid MLPs, as well. Historically, this has left the MLP group to the high net worth individual who desires significant, reliable, current income and who is undaunted by a K-1. Today, MLPs are reasonably well known and accepted by the affluent investor.

> The MLP is designed for the knowledgeable investor who seeks to control the tax liability of his portfolio income.

The MLP can be an excellent investment. It is designed for the knowledgeable investor who seeks to control the tax liability of his portfolio income. An MLP's actual distributed income is almost always higher than the taxable, reported income as a result of depreciation and other expense items. Most income from depreciating assets is deferred and thus reported when the investment is actually sold, as the depreciation reduces the cost basis. When designing an investment portfolio, MLP income can be viewed as an alternative or supplement to tax free municipal bond income. As much as 80% of the income may be tax free.

The general partner has an ongoing incentive to maintain or increase distributions each year. General partners often receive as much as 15% to 50% of the increase in net cash flow through incentive distribution rights, so they have every reason to wisely manage the resource. Leverage, while often minimal, can become excessive with some offers. Be aware of the debt-to-capital ratio and keep it reasonable: less than 50%. Of course, net income should always be paid without incurring new debt. Issuance of new preferred stock or common stock will dilute earnings sharing capabilities, at least initially. It is a common capital raising alternative to debt, but it also dilutes shareholders' earnings.

The tax reporting form is the K-1, which many CPAs recoil from due to its complexity. For your tax convenience, many MLPs keep tax records for all investors. These are typically available to you and your CPA online. Most MLPs today have the K-1s posted to their websites, some even downloadable directly to your tax preparation software. Each keeps track of your individual position. State filing requirements are often immaterial, as most MLPs transport through non-tax states such as Texas or Wyoming. If there is a potential state tax liability, the capital threshold can be significant, typically $200,000 and more.

Holding the investment for several years requires maintenance of tax records for each of those years. The limited partner may have to file a tax return for the state from which the income derives. If the investment is held in a qualified account such as an IRA or other form of retirement account, the issue of unrelated business tax income (UBTI) may arise. UBTI can be a tax nightmare for the retirement account. This is why pensions do not hold MLPs. Holding the investment in a personal qualified account—such as an IRA or a small business pension account—may eliminate the foregoing complexity, although any distributions from the qualified account are fully taxable. These tax concerns are what tend to make the asset class a neglected one. UBTI becomes a tax issue at capital thresholds in excess of $1 million, typically.

It may help to walk through a sample distribution to understand its workings. (See Figure 3.) Recall that the intent is to generate a high degree of consistent income. Assume a purchase of 1,000 shares at $20 a share, for $20,000, and a first year distribution of $2 per share or 10%—a fairly common event in the MLP world in 2010. Since 70% to 80% of distributions can be a return of principal, $.40 per share may be partnership income and taxed as ordinary income, while the remaining $1.60 may be a tax free payout. Since the $1.60 is a return of principal (through depreciation and depletion), this reduces the cost basis per share by $1.60, to $18.40. If, at the end of that year, the stock were subsequently sold for $25—an increase of $5 per share—$1.60 per share would be taxed as ordinary income and $5 per share would be taxed as long-term capital gains. Assuming the highest federal and state tax brackets, the tax load would amount to $200 + $1,250 + $800 = $2,250. Your after tax income ($2,000 minus $200) would be 9% ($1,800) and your total return would be $4,750 or 23.75%. We ignore here the "paper losses" from the MLP, which would result in further reduction in tax liability. There may also be individual state tax returns filing—but in most cases for the small investor these would be minimal and not subject to filing requirements.

If the stock is held until the cost basis is reduced to zero, any negative tax capital account would be recognized upon sale. If the security is held until the owner passes away, under current law the new step-up in cost basis would eliminate the previous tax cost accounting entirely. The price appreciation would be ignored and the price on date of death (or six months thereafter) would become the new cost basis.

Cost basis: $20,000

10% distribution: $2,000

$.40 x 1000 shares = $400 (ordinary income)

$1.60 x 1000 shares = $1,600 (return of principal)

50% combined tax = $200 on $400 of ordinary income

Deferred tax at 50% ordinary income tax: $1,600 x .50 = $800

Distribution:	$2,000
Gain on sale:	$5,000
Total pretax income:	$7,000

Sale of stock:	$25,000
Original price:	$20,000
Gain on sale:	$ 5,000
Tax on gain at 25%:	$5,000 x .25 = $1,250

$2,000 distribution

$ 200 tax

$1,800 after tax distribution

Gross proceeds:	$27,000 ($2,000 income + $5,000 gain + original basis)
Total taxes:	$ 2,250 ($200 + $1,250 + $800)
Net proceeds:	$24,750

Figure 3. Sample MLP Distribution

Working with Your CPA

When you acquire an MLP, or group of them, you need to edu-cate your CPA before tax season begins. If she is aware, she won't rattle your cage when tax prep time comes around. If she just gets the K-1(s) along with your other tax receipts, her work flow will be interrupted and you will be dressed down for making such a foolish investment. Simply tell her that you are offering her a raise—the cost of preparing a few more tax forms. She will understand, and more importantly, she should prepare her staff for the added complexity of your return. She will be mollified and you will have a portfolio return that more closely meets your retirement income objective.

The K-1 tax reporting issue can be avoided through the use of a closed-end management investment company such as that available from Tortoise Capital Advisors, Claymore Advisors, or Kayne Anderson. Tortoise has four closed-end management in-vestment companies. These are organized to provide a high level of potential total return, emphasizing current income. They in-vest in MLPs. Because they are closed-end funds, their distribu-tions are treated as dividends and taxed accordingly. The return of capital issue is essentially ignored for the investor, although still reported for those who wish to employ it. The 1099 form is used for reporting of all income and depreciation. The funds often use leverage to enhance yield, to pay their fees, and to offset potential tax liabilities. This use of debt also increases volatility and risk. The lunch is never free; you just have to choose which meal you want, with or without your CPA at the table.

The funds above are designed for the institutional and quali-fied investor, for example, the IRA. Each fund holds a diversi-fied group of MLPs from the minerals distribution world and offers similar yields. They employ leverage in the acquisition and management of their funds, which impacts their cost structure. The management fee varies between .95% and 1.5%. Inclusive of leverage costs, they describe their total annual expenses—as a percent of total managed assets—as falling in a range of 2.7% to 2.9%.[1] For that fee you hold a full house of MLPs and pay the fund for their expertise. Each fund has varying characteristics, yields, and performance, so each must be viewed within the usual context of risk, competitors, experience, and cost. Your net yield is impacted by the fee; 10% becomes 8.5% and 7% becomes 5.5% at a 1.5% fee. The performance is a result of the underlying MLPs. The risk may be less, or greater, than investing in individual MLPs.

Risk Issues

As with any investment offering income as a major component, interest rate risk is prevalent with an MLP. The risk can become significant when the yield component is higher than the sector average or higher than the market in general. If interest rates rise, the value of existing securities with a known yield may drop. For example, if the "risk free" return from a newly issued US Treasury bond was 7%, rather than today's 3.25%, other securities offering a return of 7% would decline in value to compensate for the perceived risk relative to the (supposedly) risk free Treasury. The yield of those devalued securities would thus increase, to reward their holders for the higher risk. An MLP offering a 7% distribution might decline in value by 15% to 20% as a result of such a scenario, and concurrently, its yield would increase for the new buyer. Any growth potential may add value to the price of the MLP, also. Growth could be the result of business enterprise activity, market perception, product value enhancement, or general economic recovery.

MLPs can be subject to financial risk, as they have minimal retained earnings, since they have to pass through more than 90% of their net income. Their balance sheet forces them to expand by taking on new debt or new equity issuance. This can put MLPs at the mercy of private investors, the debt or equity marketplaces, or all three. As private equity can be a favorite source of capital in the energy world, CEOs of MLPs do want to sit with their backs to the wall when playing cards with these good old boys. The industries of energy extraction, transportation, storage, and distribution is a direct, purposeful offshoot of the integrated oils. They are the players in the field which have spun off most of the MLPs. In addition, acquisition and consolidation strategies are in play today. The largest MLPs are on the prowl to acquire more pipeline and storage facilities. The individual investor wants to know who is attempting an acquisition by following the websites of the investments and the financial media. The investor does not have a say in the game, but he does have a play in the game: he can walk away from a company's stock if he becomes uncomfortable. There are many players in the game.

Management risk should also be taken into consideration. Management of a company is nearly always critical to its failure. It is less critical to its success. An exploitive management team can wreak destruction on a firm and leave it vulnerable for many years, if not entirely destroyed. Humility in success is a rare find in executives. Compensation concerns have recently led to the proposed legislation taxing excessive carry trade. Members of the House may judge this to be a form of income for the management team and tax it as ordinary income, rather than capital gain.

Regulatory risk can be another potential danger. The interstate transportation of gases is regulated by the Federal Energy Regulatory Commission (FERC), a politicized organization that has twice this century changed the indexing methodology for pipeline pricing. One could easily imagine a host of reasons to further change, alter, or abolish the regulatory issues underlying the transportation of gases interstate. Environmental issues can have an impact, either positively or negatively. If carbon credits become a required aspect of the industry, the extension of regulatory authority will ensue.

Energy demand will always change as society's perception of its needs, sources, and types of energy change. The assumption built in to most national energy use models is for an annual increase in energy use of 1% for the US. The current recession has impacted that figure, perhaps temporarily. Demand can and does shift among the energy sources. Natural gas has become far more available, reliable and environmentally acceptable during the first decade of the 21st century. The Marcellus and Bakken fields have made the US the largest exploiter of natural gas in the world. Extensive carbon regulation and taxation is currently a legislative and regulatory consideration. How these changes impact the transportation and storage of fuel types may alter the markets' perception of value in each MLP. It is just as easy to foresee an increase in demand as it is to foresee an increase in regulation. Whether net distributions increase or not is a risk the investor takes.

The systemic risk that markets suffered through during the winter of 2008-2009 destroyed values across the spectrum of the investment universe. Few foresaw it; fewer still acted preventatively. Virtually all participants lost. Only time will tell whether or not increased regulation will act as a prophylactic against this form of risk. You are responsible for managing your wealth, or for working with someone to whom you delegate this responsibility. Stop-loss programs can help to ameliorate these losses.

There are many points of view about market risk. Modern portfolio theory is one. If we accept its premises for the current discussion, MLPs present an opportunity for greater diversification. The MLP world could be viewed as an asset class—it certainly is a subset of the energy industry. Even if one does not consider this small universe as an asset class, it does offer the|opportunity for further diversification. The MLP returns show very low correlation to most other asset classes, as shown in the graph from DiMeo Schneider and Associates.

Performance of MLPs vs Other Asset Classes

Asset Class	Total Return 1990-2010 annualized
MLP	16.4%
REIT	10.7%
US Small Cap Equities	9.2%
US Large Cap Equities	8.8%
Investment Grade Bonds	7.5%
High Yield Bonds	6.1%
Municipal Bonds	6.1%
International Equities	4.2%
Treasury Bills	3.7%

Figure 4. MLP Returns

The MLP Index has less than .3 beta with any class of assets other than high yield bonds. That is, it fluctuates in value far less than the market itself; the correlation is quite low. This can have the dual effect of increased returns and lower volatility. Note that these references apply in general; in a systemic risk environment such as the winter of 2008-2009, all asset classes perform in tandem. Recall the complexity issue.

BUSINESS DEVELOPMENT CORPORATIONS (BDCS)

The more complex the investment, the less a portion of it, if any, belongs in a portfolio. A significant amount of knowledge must be garnered to make good decisions about complicated securities. Business development companies (BDCs) are a clear case in point. They have the potential for high dividends. In exchange, you have the responsibility to know as much about them as you can and monitor their behavior if you are going to use them in your portfolio.

In 1980 Congress passed the Small Business Investment Incentive Act. The new law authorized the establishment of business development companies. The intent was to provide capital and managerial expertise to small firms without access to public capital markets. Thus BDCs lend capital to, or take an equity position in, small companies who repay the debt with interest, stock, and dividends—as well as repayment of the principal. If there is a capital event—that is, if the firm goes public—the BDC expects significant gain from their equity exposure.

BDCs actively seek to take managerial control and offer expansion direction. They offer lending facilities, take equity positions, and provide consulting services. They can raise up to $5 million each year in "free trading stock" (stock that is exempt from SEC registration). Their debt-to-equity ratio cannot be larger than 200%. They must provide or offer significant managerial assistance.

What BDCs Offer and How They Work

BDCs are closed-end investment firms, as defined by the Investment Company Act of 1940, operating as venture capital companies. They are typically organized as limited partnerships, for the pass-through of tax treatment. Some have been established as corporations under subchapter M of the IRS. They either lend to or take an equity position in the firms under consideration. They cannot own more than 10% of any company's voting securities. They cannot place more than 5% of their assets in any one security. They cannot have more than 25% of their total assets in businesses they control or in businesses that are in the same industry.

To maintain their status they must distribute at least 90% of their investment company taxable income: the dividends, interest, and payments in kind that they receive each year as a result of their capital practices. Although first designed in 1980, they were insignificant (with the exception of Allied Capital), with less than $1 billion in assets until 2004, when the first IPOs came to market. A rapid-fire splattering of a dozen or more hit the wires in a few months. Today BDCs have more than $23 billion in assets, divided among more than two dozen firms.

There are significant differences between externally managed and internally managed BDCs:

- The internal management fees are generally higher with an externally managed BDC.
- Externally managed BDCs have a registered investment advisor as the managing firm, while internally managed BDCs have their own directors, executives, and managers, whose compensation can be directly tied to the performance of the underlying investments.
- Most of the IPOs since 2004 are externally managed.
- Conflicts of interest between the manager and the BDC owner tend to be fewer with an internally managed BDC.

+ Your capital gains participation potential is far greater with an internally managed BDC.

Thus, the few internally managed BDCs may be your first considerations.

Mezzanine financing is the BDC's typical approach. This is financing whose seniority is below senior debt but above common or preferred equity. It usually has an equity kicker as a component, to boost the potential total return and compensate for the greater risk as a subordinated loan. The equity can be in the form of warrants, rights, or performance fees. The repayment of the debt is typically treated as a return of principal to the BDC, rather than as a taxable dividend. Equity finance looks better on the balance sheet of a company—the receiver of the funds from the BDC—and is more acceptable to its possible current lenders. The warrants or rights are usually subject to anti-dilution rights, to protect the holder—the BDC—but the ways around this are limitless.

BDCs lend against equipment, plant, inventory, and receivables. This puts them in the senior-most position for payment. It also puts them 30 days away from taking over any company to which they offer this capital. These are big boys who know the game of finance. If they loan your firm capital, you had better be sure you can pay it back. Miss a payment and they will seize the asset in 15 days. You, the struggling young CEO, will become very quickly unemployed, perhaps without a house or car. These boys play it big and they play it tough. As an investor, you like having this clout. As a borrower, you turn to them as a last resort.

At least 90% of the BDC income has to be distributed to the shareholders. They can pay significant dividends. Because they must be invested in a variety of companies, they are often quite diversified, particularly the largest BDCs. They have a vested interest in the success of the firms they invest in, so they can be viewed as partners with you.

BDCs offer a way to indirectly invest in private equity without the legal and regulatory expense—and without the high qualification limits imposed by the SEC for such investments. They are liquid—as liquid as the markets in which they trade.

BDC Risks

How do you evaluate the BDC world and its many participants? Let's explore some of them in more detail. Here are a few of the obvious risks.[2]

Expenses are outrageously high. These folks think they know a few things and are not shy about charging a premium fee for their expertise and knowledge. An externally managed BDC has performance fees—in addition to management fees—which together can erode most capital gains potential. In addition, leverage costs can add up when interest rates climb.

The potential for conflicts of interest abound. The management firm for an external may have an incentive to offer better opportunities to their institutional or high net worth clients versus their public clients. They may or may not be judicious in their division of the equity participation in a company that has excellent prospects. You are dependent upon their good faith.

Failure is a perennial risk. The companies receiving the investment capital are small companies. These are the lifeblood of the nation. As employers they hold 65% and more of the workforce in the US. They are the cradle from which will emerge the next Netflix and Google. Their failure rate can approach 90%, depending upon the industry, the executive's experience and personal wealth, timing, regulatory challenges and opportunities, the state of the economy, burn rate, and a host of other factors.

Liquidity risk applies to the equity markets within which their stock is traded. As with the preferred stock market, the nefarious debt instruments of the last few years, and frankly with all markets, systemic risk can freeze a market or markets. The result can be a devastating blow to your stock through no fault of the stock itself. Stop losses prevail in offering some shelter from these storms.

What to Look for in a BDC

You want to know that the BDC principals have skin in the game. Internals do, by definition. Externals may have skin, or may not have much of it at all. You would like to see the management team taking board positions in the firms to which they lend. The concentration into any company or industry should lie within the regulatory envelope. The BDC should be investing in a variety of industries; some focus on just one. If you like that industry, fine; follow the BDC on their website. The dividend should be fully supported by the cash flow, as with any of our suggestions. Free cash flow is a paramount selector, especially with BDCs. A return of principal as a result of a new equity offering is against your wishes. You want a return upon your principal.

You can follow each of the BDCs on their websites. Quantumonline.com is an excellent choice for information, as is wallstreet.com. Read their prospectuses. The investments they make can be quite interesting to you, but don't fall in love with any.

How to Invest in a BDC

As a suggested guideline, 4% to 6% of a portfolio may be invested in BDCs, once you get up to speed. You are doing so for the enhanced yield. In exchange for putting a potential of 5% of your

---

MLPs and BDCs can turbo charge your portfolio's income generation.

---

portfolio at considerable risk (with the usual 10% stop loss!), you may be earning 9% to 10%. The expected result to your income stream is the same as having twice as much invested in another vehicle with a return of 4.5% to 5%. Any upside potential is gravy. Fifty thousand dollars invested here has the same impact on your distribution as $100,000 invested in stocks earning 5%.

Because the distributions are not dividends but capital gains or return of principal, consider these for your tax-deferred or qualified accounts. If you use these in a non-qualified account, the tax reporting can be cumbersome for your CPA, so alert her before tax season comes around. If the BDC has a change in its investments, fees, results, or stock price, you need to seriously consider bailing on it. These stocks warrant your time. You need to pay attention to the details. If you were a growth investor, these would be the highest risk aspects of your portfolio, the drivers of growth. View them as the potential drivers of your income strategy.

In Conclusion

MLPs and BDCs can turbo charge your portfolio's income generation. Assigning 15% to 18% of the total portfolio to these two categories can possibly drive the total distribution yield beyond the 7% objective. A close monitoring of the stocks you choose is necessary, as with any security selection, but especially with these investments. Attractive features include: tax advantaged income for the sophisticated investor, historically low volatility of stock price, low correlation to other sectors and industries and correlation well below the market itself, low debt-to-equity ratios, volatility well below that of the marketplace itself, nominal short positions, significant free cash flow figures, sustainable distributions, and high yield potential.

WORKSHEET

Assignment: Explore helpful websites.

Visit the following websites. Spend as much time as you can at each site, learning, discovering, and experimenting. If the site interests you, subscribe.

MLPs
Quantumonline.com
Naptp.org
ipaa.org
dividenddetective.com

BDCs
Bdcs.valueforum.com

Once you are familiar with the concepts, go to the sites and read up on the companies that interest you. You are getting into more advanced research, so take your time, take notes, and go for walks!

10

OTHER INCOME SOURCES: REAL ESTATE, REITS, BUSINESS BUYOUTS AND STRUCTURED SETTLEMENTS

> "Price is what you pay. Value is what you get."
>
> **—Warren Buffet**

The total estimated value of all US real estate—commercial, industrial, land and residential—is approximately that of the US stock market: $12 trillion. Each has declined by more than $4 trillion in the past two years. There happens to be another $12 trillion in cash and cash equivalents in banks, money markets, CDs, etc. We can surmise that real estate, like cash, is at least as important as the stock markets.

PRIVATELY HELD REAL ESTATE

Our primary real estate holding is our home. Nearly 65% of us own our own home, in conjunction with the lender who fronted us the mortgage. Many of our Baby Boom generation own our homes outright, with no debt—more than 60% of us. A significant number of us own another property, typically a second home or a rental property. If we have been smart about it, we have rented it out, at least some of the time, in the case of our second home or vacation home. The rent we receive helps to pay the mortgage, taxes, insurance, utilities, and repairs on the property.

Rental Real Estate in the Retirement Portfolio

As property owners, we get to enjoy the free cash flow of rental income. We get to keep this cash flow. The Schedule D that we use to file our tax return upon the property also allows a deduction for depreciation. This figure, taken each year as a portion of the original acquisition price, is itemized as an expense against income. It is a bookkeeping item. It has no real cost to us each year. Depreciation allows us to keep a portion of the income from the property without taxation. It shelters the income. It gives us tax free income.

This net income is ours to use as we wish. It may have been the most important reason for purchasing the property. If so, then we clearly should regard the rental as another income producing asset. We can compare the net cash with the capital we invested and determine the rate of return upon that capital. For example, if we have a total capital outlay (purchase cost plus capital expenses) of $150,000 and if we have net annual income of $12,000, then we are earning 8% on the real estate ($12,000 divided by $150,000 = .08). This compares well with the dividend received from a 7% dividend yielding security.

We now have another asset to support us in retirement. Of course, you the owner have known this for years, but it bears repeating. Many financial advisors tend to ignore this asset in their retirement cash flow analysis for you. If you are comfortable with the responsibilities as landlord or with your management company, the asset should continue to offer good, strong, free cash flow. You also understand that vacancies affect cash flow, as do maintenance and upgrades.

It is important to recognize the difference between current value and capital invested when you compute the rate of return. Even today, if you have owned the property for more than a decade, it has appreciated beyond what you paid for it. You probably didn't buy it for all cash. You have certainly paid down the note it carries. If the net cash flow is divided by the current value, your rate of return is much lower than if it is factored by your capital outlay. For example, if the property is worth $500,000, the $12,000 net income is less than a 2.5% "dividend." This is a false bogey. You would have to pay a realtor's commission, settlement costs, the remaining mortgage, taxes, and perhaps something to "show" the asset. A truer comparison is the rate of return you might expect (let's just say 7%!) from the net proceeds of a sale versus the current yield on your invested capital.

> The challenge of real estate ownership is its illiquid market.

The challenge of real estate ownership, of course, is its illiquid market. The value "trapped" inside the property should thus reflect a premium for the imbalance of the market—its illiquidity. You should expect a slightly greater rate of return from real estate than from a similarly liquid investment to compensate you for the liquidity risk.

Improving Your Real Estate Investment Return

How can you improve on this 2.5%? You could pay down the debt further, or pay it off. After a few decades of profligate credit access, we as a nation are beginning to pay down our personal debt. We are doing so at a prodigious rate. If you have excess cash in a bank CD earning less than 2.5%, it may be better utilized by reducing the debt on the property.

Let's use a new example. If you have a CD for $100,000 earning 2.5% in a one-year time deposit and have $100,000 in debt on your rental property—valued at $150,000 with a 5% mortgage for 15 more years—then it may behoove you to reposition the cash and eliminate the debt. By so doing, you can increase your net income and have a significant portion of it come to you tax free as a result of depreciation.

The loan cost is $536.82 monthly or $6,441.84 a year. You eliminate the loan cost by paying off the debt. The $536.82 increases your income—your "dividend" from the asset. You would now be earning 4.4% on your $150,000 capital. Since you have the luxury of the Schedule D, the depreciation will allow you to shelter a portion of that income—typically one-third of it, if you are in a 28% federal and 5% state effective tax bracket. Your net after-tax income goes up to $7,331.03.

By the way, you would have paid taxes on the annual $2,500 in CD interest. At the same 33% combined tax rate, you would keep just $1,675 after the tax haircut. Compare that to the $7,331.03. You win.

You would do this only if you had other cash, in other deposits. You will always want to maintain a comfortable cash reserve cushion for emergencies or for opportunities. You must consider whether it is wise to invest this cash into real estate. You are putting capital into an asset that has recently declined in value substantially. Only you can decide whether you think it will continue to perform as a wasting asset or will appreciate again. If you had to access the capital in the building, you would have to go through the loan process again: applying, being appraised, possibly paying more in taxes, loan costs, interest rate risk, etc.

The Depreciation Factor

When we sell the property, we have to reduce our acquisition cost by the amount of depreciation we have previously taken. Section 172 forces us to reduce our cost basis by the amount of depreciation we have taken over the years of ownership in the real property. This will have a *very* significant effect upon us, tax-wise, if we have held the property for many years. If you have owned a rental property for more than fifteen years, your cost basis has been reduced by nearly half of your acquisition cost. Let's use our previous capital investment of $150,000. If half of the capital has been depreciated, when you sell, that amount will reduce your capital base to $75,000. Your gain will be computed upon this value, rather than on the $150,000. Alternatives to an outright sale might be a 1031 exchange or a charitable contribution of the property, either outright or to a remainder or lead trust.

There are rarely simple answers to any financial question. It does make sense to evaluate your choices at retirement and make informed decisions.

Sales and 1031 Exchanges

If you are fed up with the hassles of being a landlord, you have to consider your many choices. You can sell the rental, pay taxes, and put the money in the bank. You can gift the rental to a charitable remainder trust, as we will discuss in the next chapter. You do reap significant income and tax rewards in exchange for a deferred gift to your church or nonprofit. You can also exchange the property for one of similar type and of equal or greater value.

The 1031 exchange process, as this is called, can be complex. It can also be lucrative when done properly. As with any game, the more complex the rules, the better off the player who is well prepared. The benefits of a 1031 exchange are:

- deferred taxation on the depreciated asset
- an increase in your net income
- retirement from the exciting world of being a landlord.

The following guidelines must be followed to accord with the 1031 section of the Internal Revenue Code:

- The exchange must be of a like kind: both properties must be held for a productive purpose in business or trade.
- The exchange must go through the hands of a qualified intermediary (QI); you cannot have constructive receipt of the capital at any time.
- The acquired property must be encumbered by debt of the same or higher amount relative to their respective equity.
- You have exactly 45 calendar days, without exception, to identify the property or properties for the exchange.
- You have exactly 180 calendar days to complete the transaction.

These rules are to be followed strictly. You do need the advice of a competent financial advisor, CPA, qualified intermediary, attorney, and realtor to enter into and to complete the process. This is a game with very stringent rules. Follow them and you can win. Ignore them at your peril.

The exchange can be to another property or properties that you have chosen, if you wish to keep your hand in the property management game. If you wish to exit property management, then the 1031 property list is composed of those available from a non-traded REIT firm, such as Inland, Cole, REI, etc. There are a few exchange specialists in the real estate market. Use them once you have interviewed them. Their goal—in addition to making money off of your money—is to "season" the properties for the institutional market. A new property is placed into an exchange, tenants are found, the property is managed for at least five years, then sold to institutional investors. They want to buy a premium property with a track record. Ideally, you have provided it.

These sponsors hold the property in an LLC or as a TIC—tenants in common. Your legal advisor will detail the differences for you. These are typically qualified properties. That means you must be a qualified investor. A qualified investor is one who has income of at least $200,000 for the past three years, has a net worth of more than $2 million, excluding your home, and for whom the exchange represents less than 50% of their net worth, excluding their home. There are usually only 35 investors in the property; there can be fewer but no more than this number.

If there is a liquidity event, these 35 "members" are the first market to turn to for resale. For example, once you have passed away, your estate may want to sell the interest inherited. The trustee or administrator of the estate would offer the interest to the other 34 members. If they all refuse, then it can be offered to members of the public. If anyone wishes to buy, a price must be agreed upon. This means an appraisal, certainly. The sales proceeds are then deposited to the estate account for further distribution to heirs, claimants, etc. This is exactly what would happen for any piece of real property. The significant difference is the small size of the market.

As you can see, the rules are strict and complex. You need, and pay for, the advice of experts in this field. Enter into this type of arrangement only with firms of significant experience. Evaluate closely the value of the end result versus your cost of entry. It may mean that an outright sale makes as much sense, or more. You also must be comfortable giving up management control of the new property. For many, that would be a blessing; for some it means loss of control. This decision is to be made only after long and serious consideration. The tax and income benefits, while significant, are only a portion of the equation.

Brainstorming Income Producing Real Estate Ideas

Now that you are thinking about real estate, you may come up with a few ideas of your own. How about renting out a vacation yacht in the Caribbean? Some of the more esoteric income producers were outlined in a recent *Wall Street Journal* article. These included railway rights of way, parking meters, cell phone towers, student housing, and self-storage facilities. Income streams from these rarefied investments were listed in the high single digits: 6% to 9% annual yield. Nice job if you can get it. They typify the incredible animus of the entrepreneurs who make up this fabled land.

You have to know the territory. If you have the drive to pursue your own real estate investment type, more power to you! There are, according to Brent Hayes of Athens County, Ohio, more than 100,000 miles of abandoned rail beds in the US. In addition to the value of the real estate beneath the railways and adjacent to them, the gravel, ties, and the rail itself have commercial worth. If you have the interest in pursuing these opportunities, you also have the dexterity and gumption to deal with the environment folks and legal constraints that may stand in your way. Putting up a cell tower on your roof may be more to your liking. The majority of self-storage facilities are still owned by private firms, unlike the listed properties from such heavyweights as Public Storage.

Who hasn't considered buying a home or condo when their teenagers begin considering college? The kids manage it and live there, thus teaching them good business sense—and perhaps finally instilling cleanliness habits. You, hopefully, have a tax break and perhaps a slightly positive cash flow from the unit. Some years later you sell the property to another parent.

REAL ESTATE INVESTMENT TRUSTS (REITs)

If managing property is not your idea of fun, you can still enjoy ownership in the real estate asset class by investing in a real estate investment trust (REIT).

REITs and What They Offer

A real estate investment trust (REIT) is a company that owns—and in most cases operates—income-producing real estate. Like securities, the shares of many REITS are traded on major stock exchanges. Shares in a REIT are called units.

To qualify as a REIT, a company must have most of its assets and income tied to real estate investment and must distribute at least 90% of its taxable income to shareholders annually in the form of dividends. A company that qualifies as a REIT is permitted to deduct dividends paid to its shareholders from its corporate taxable income. As a result, most REITs distribute all of their taxable income to their shareholders so they do not have to pay corporate tax on earnings.

Most REITs invest in the equity in real property, some in mortgages, and some in both. Those that invest in equities historically have performed better than those that have invested in mortgage-backed real estate. The risks in the publicly traded mortgage market were amply demonstrated to us from 2007 to 2010. Leverage drives yield and our drive here is away from excess leverage. Buyer beware.

REITs generally purchase properties that produce income. Most of the profits earned are passed on to investors in the form of dividends. REITs may typically own apartment buildings, shopping malls, hotels, restaurant chains, commercial office buildings, hospitality (hotels), student housing, prisons, and even cemeteries.

Advantages of Owning a REIT

REITs provide a way for you to invest in commercial real estate without incurring the expense of buying an entire office building or fast food restaurant and without the responsibility of managing it. To use our earlier example, if you'd like to avoid the hassle of managing a condo for your college-age kid, you can invest in a student housing REIT.

REITS offer many other advantages as well. Diversity of holdings usually spreads risk over many geographical areas and industries. REITS offer liquidity—you can buy them as stock, preferreds, unit investment trusts (UITs), electronically traded funds (ETFs), or in mutual funds and variable annuities.

> REITS offer liquidity and can serve as a hedge against inflation.

Because depreciation shelters the income stream from a REIT, you might want to consider this investment for your taxable or non-qualified accounts. These regular dividends can be distributed to you as income or reinvested to purchase additional stock.

Although there is no guarantee that property values will rise, real estate has historically served as a hedge against inflation. The same can be true of your REIT holdings. Thus, real estate may hedge your portfolio against the inflationary pressures of excessively loose monetary policy or significant price increases resulting from public demand. As we saw in 2007 through 2011, real estate can also be subject to incredible downward pressure with market-wide systemic risk, with recessionary declines in demand, and with rent-seeking investment banks creating complex investment products loosely linked back to an invisible porridge of questionable real estate debt. Tread lightly here.

A portion of a portfolio invested in REITs can offer some income advantage if the underlying properties have less than 50% debt in the form of mortgages. You should seek yields of 5% to 8% and will discover this range during most parts of the economic cycle. Buying REITs after several years of price appreciation and acquiring 4% to 5% yields on your capital can be a recipe for disaster. Buying REITs during a recession and achieving yields of 8% to 12% can be a decade-long reward for patience. Under these circumstances, you may find that 8% to 15% of your portfolio here invested can drive the overall portfolio yield upwards by a quarer point: .25%. As with any equity position, the 10% stop loss banner should fly high. Be prepared to take your lumps if you make a mistake. "Fail early, fail often" is the phrase in the private equity world of Silicon Valley.

Other Considerations

If you own units in a REIT, you must pay taxes on the dividends received and also on any capital gains. Like MLPs, REITs use the K-1 tax reporting form.

As with any investment, market factors can affect your REIT investment. For example, if mortgage rates rise, the value of a mortgage REIT will be less, reducing your potential return on investment. This can quickly decimate the value of such a security, as many are leveraged to enhance yield. These are for others to own, rather than you.

Even if the REIT you own invests only in all-cash real estate, if vacancies increase and gross margins decline, profits will go down and so, in turn, will your dividends.

In summary, whether you hold the full deed on a property or simply a few shares in a REIT, real estate can contribute to the yield in your 7% portfolio. As with any investment, you'll want to view real estate through the spectacles of risk, taxes, yield, and personal tolerance.

BUSINESS BUYOUTS

If you are a business owner, you have spent blood and treasure in building it up from an idea to where it is today. This beast, this lover, this creature of wealth has become your child. It is the means by which you have escaped the daily grind and a source of pride. You also made a pretty penny at it. You are doing what you do well.

When you retire, you will either sell it or continue to run it. If the latter, then you may step back a bit each year, turning over the daily operations, or the marketing, to another. It may be a family member—perhaps your son or daughter, who has been involved since a teenager. They have an obvious gusto for the career and you are beginning to be willing to let some of it go to them. Yes, it isn't easy letting go. They understand, as they mature, the secret joy of selling, of manufacturing, or of designing. Once in the blood, this passion doesn't disappear. Still, you can walk away slowly, giving more control to others, allowing yourself time for different distractions and attractions.

On the other hand, you may be fed up with the beast. Enough already! You know a few competitors who would love to take over their best champion and increase their market share and their odds. If you plan to sell, you have to have a market, a price, funding, and some sort of guaranty. When you sell, you end up with some combination of capital and annual income—in most cases. You have significant tax consequences. You have to make capital decisions that you probably have never made before.

While this text is intended to discuss income sources and their use, the transactions involved in the sale of a business are for another storyteller. Dini, Steingold, and Crosier are three authors with excellent reference texts on the subject. You could do worse than read each of these in preparation for the event. The basic issues are listed below.

- Preparing the firm for sale
- Evaluating and appraising
- Discovering the buyer
- Understanding tax complications and requirements
- Limiting your liability
- Clarifying your current and future relationship with the prospective buyer
- Working with attorneys, accountants, and brokers
- Negotiating, closing, and transferring
- Deciding what to do with the proceeds

Your legal and tax advisor had better know the complexities of the deal. Read and study in anticipation of the meetings with each of them. Well prepared, you can make the best use of their time and expertise. You can also determine their level of knowledge and exploit it to your best advantage. If they are not keen to the task, ask them who is. This is one of the top five most important decisions of your life (marriage, children, health, retirement and the others). You get one chance to do it right. You may wish to consult a business broker, but ascertain that he is a member of the association. Anyone can be such a broker with a little accounting skill. A few actually know what they are doing. You will pay 10% of the sales price to them, typically. Be sure it is worth your time!

The retirement challenges here are of income and of taxation:

+ How will you take the sales proceeds—over time, or in a lump sum?
+ What will be the tax consequences?

The answers to these two questions will make your retirement flush or flushed, feast or famine. Each is tied to the other. We have no idea what the tax brackets and rates will be in two years or in ten years. If you think they will be higher in the future, then you may want to take more capital up front and pay at a "lower" rate. If you think that the rates will be the same or lower because, for example, your income will be less, then you may want to attenuate the payment schedule. How the tax is applied is important. Is the capital received for your share of the business taxed as capital gains (what is the basis?), ordinary income, recaptured Section 179, or return of principal? It probably will be a combination of all of the above.

Can you gift shares to other family members prior to the sale? Can you gift to a charity or to your family foundation? Does the new owner want you to remain on board for a period of time to ensure proper training, continuity, and retention of client bases? Does he want a no compete clause for a number of years? Does that matter to you? If it is a small firm, can you sell it to the employees? If it is a large and very successful firm, what are the capital structure choices?

All of these play into your decision to sell. The net proceeds will support a degree of lifestyle perhaps imagined when first you opened the doors, so many years ago. The devil will be in the detail—value, price, time frame, net income. You've done well. End it well.

STRUCTURED SETTLEMENTS

Structured settlements can be anything from the lottery win to the divorce decree to the wrongful death settlement to a viaticum in anticipation of premature death. Unfortunately, only the first is any fun.

A settlement is a legal event. It is the contract entered into and agreed upon by two or more parties. They are rarely private. They are enforced by the court of jurisdiction.

In the rare event that you receive a structured settlement, it can be an important aspect of your retirement. While the odds of winning the lottery or receiving a large lump sum due to an unexpected tragedy are rather small, you do need to know what to do if the event arises.

If you are in a settlement discussion, you need to have the advantage of a competent attorney. You also need to consult with a tax advisor to discuss the tax ramifications of the settlement or, lucky you, the lottery winnings. If you do win a lottery, you need to consult with a lottery legal advisor about your choices for receiving distribution, provided there are choices in your state. You should also consider delisting you phone number and keeping the fact to yourself. The woodwork will crawl with family, friends, associates, business advisors, and all other crackpots wishing to part you from your winnings. They will succeed if you listen to them. Go away for a few weeks to quiet down the traffic.

These unlikely situations, when they do arise, are unique. You have faced other challenges, but quite unlike this. Seek guidance, privately. Get a second and third opinion. Make your decisions slowly and with deliberation. You know this already. Just as you were taught by your folks, slow and steady wins the race.

WORKSHEET

Assignment: Explore helpful websites.

Visit the following websites. Spend as much time as you can at each site, learning, discovering, and experimenting. Subscribe to those that interest you.

REIT.com.
bizbuysell.com
IRA.gov
lifesettlements.dealflow.com

11

DESIGNING THE 7% PORTFOLIO

Now that you've been debriefed on the various potential elements of your 7% portfolio—stocks, bonds, preferreds, ETFs, CEFs, MLPs, BDCs, real estate, REITs, business buyouts, and structured settlements—we'll discuss how you might put them together to create the income you'll need in retirement.

One of the intrinsic beauties of this 7% approach to portfolio design is this:

> *Your portfolio's return is not measured against the market.*
> *It is measured against your annual income need.*

Think about that. You are free from the vicissitudes of tracking the market, beating the market, or outperforming your peer group. Frankly, you could care less how you perform versus a public benchmark. Your definition of success is: Have you met your income goal? Are you enjoying retirement?

You are not tied to a benchmark, the market, or your wife's best friend's cousin, Vinnie. How they do is immaterial to your success. You might even define success as how little time you have to spend doing the work of portfolio management. Your silence during a dinner party is evidence of satisfaction—and perhaps a little humility.

Success is defined by many as, "How well did your portfolio do as compared to the market?" (Pick one: the DOW, S&P 500, NASDAQ, EAFE.) In the portfolio we are building here, success is defined as, "How well did you meet your income benchmark?" An adequate return is your aspiration. That is what your forty or more years of retirement needs. That is the objective. Some years will yield a surfeit of gain; others will be leaner. Consistency in meeting your income needs is your objective. Performance against a market is irrelevant.

The approach to retirement income planning taken here is distinctly different from many other approaches. This is a "bottoms up" answer: the answer is derived from your personal financial situation. Each of you will answer this question in a slightly different way. Each of you will bring a set of tools to the task. Each of you will draw upon your knowledge and upon your experience.

Virtually all other answers are top down; they answer the question from the point of view of the marketplace, of a theory, or of an academic description. What follows is another way! This is different. This is new. All of our investment lives we have been taught that growth is important. Now we must turn away from that mantra. Now we must listen to another song. This shift takes some time to understand.

Don't Let Fear Stop You

Fear stops far too many reasonably intelligent investors from taking their portfolios into their own hands. What if I make a bad choice? What if something happens to the stock or bond company I select? What if interest rates rise? What if the market tanks? What if, what if, what if? We'll discuss risk management in more detail in the next chapter, but for now, take heart in this: by eliminating risky investments during the selection phase, by spreading the risk over a number of securities and a period of time, and by employing the 10% stop loss tool, your 7% portfolio is less likely to underperform than that overpriced and underperforming mutual fund.

Portfolio Management:
More Rewarding than Rearranging Your Spice Rack

Your 7% portfolio will never be on autopilot. There is no automatic system to monitor and assure success. Your occasional human intervention—or that of your financial advisor—is both a necessary and sufficient condition. You need to be able to design, implement, and maintain your retirement portfolio—or hire a financial professional who will meet your needs (and not expect you to meet his!). This process requires work. It lacks simplicity. Formulas for success are absent.

Should you decide, after reading the next two chapters, that portfolio design and management is more work than you care to take on, understanding the principles here will make you a far better supervisor of the financial planner you do hire. If you're going to pay her $5,000 or more each year to warm that $500,000 nest egg you're hatching, wouldn't you at least like to have an idea of what she's doing with your money?

If you have the inclination to maintain your portfolio during retirement, you certainly should have the time. As a retiree, you can spend only so much time re-arranging the spice racks in the kitchen before your spouse discharges you from that duty! The work here is not difficult. It will, however, take some time to set up. You do have to want to do this.

> **The work here is not difficult. It will, however, take some time.**

The design process is the most important. As with anything else you do, design is at least 80% of the game. Approach this as you would your workbench, your kitchen, or your toolshed. The assets you manage should be so structured as to help you meet your retirement income objective. As we have discussed, defining that objective realistically can be challenging. The examples offered in this chapter should help you come closer to a realistic number.

Maintaining the portfolio will require flexibility and judgment. Your annual income needs will change. So should your portfolio distribution. When you need fewer funds for income in a particular year, take less from the portfolio, allowing the unused income portion to reinvest for the future. As your income needs increase, take some of the portfolio income to support the need. As you find you need less, sharing of your wealth with others may become more important. We will discuss the mechanics of portfolio maintenance in greater detail in the following chapter.

Portfolio Design: Where to Begin?

How do you make sound financial decisions about the contents of your 7% portfolio? As in any purchase decision, you begin by examining the product. Whether it's a stock, a bond, or other, you look into its construction and ask pertinent questions. How does it work? What are its parts? Who makes decisions? What is revealed by its historical data? Why do you want it? When can it go wrong? The answers to these questions provide you with information.

Once you've gathered all the pertinent information, then you have to make a decision. How you make that decision is based not only upon the facts you have garnered, but also upon the totality of experience you bring to the process. It is a subjective decision based upon objective facts.

> *The facts are the guidelines for the decision;*
> *they are not the decision itself.*

As was pointed out in Chapter 5, you choose a stock, bond, or other vehicle because you've studied its features and facts. The investment makes sense to you. You do not choose it because the facts speak for themselves! You make a conscious act to accept the risk of ownership, in anticipation of the reward of ownership. It is your responsibility.

For example, suppose you are shopping for a stock. You note that the stock in question has returned at least 6% for the past 20 years. Furthermore, the company has made a dividend distribution of 3% for 18 of the past 20 years. The firm is headed by a seasoned board of directors in an industry that has been thriving. In this example, the yield, dividend, board members, and health of the industry are facts that will guide your decision. They are not foregone conclusions. You use these facts to assist you with the decision to buy. Facts and figures are aids to decisions. They are part of the process. Each of these aspects of the company will change over time.

Some Basic Arithmetic and Hypothetical Portfolio #1

Now for some basic arithmetic—some number crunching. This won't be difficult, it won't be long, and it will be easy. Remember, the numbers are metrics—tools for measurement—not tools of decision making. This distinction is the most important point here. If you do not get it, reread the previous paragraphs. Email the author. Know that the facts are simply tools, nothing more.

Add the following together: 6 + 8 = 14. Divide that by the number in the series (2). You get 7. This is the incredibly complex math behind this text. If you can net 6% interest from the bond portion of your portfolio and can net 8% in dividends from the equity half of your portfolio, your net distribution rate will be 7%.

Let's look at the bond side. If you acquired today a series of institutional quality bonds of intermediate maturities, their yields to maturity might be: 5.2%, 5.5%, 5.8%, 6%, 6.1%, 6.3%, 6.5%, and 6.6%. Add this series together. You get 48. Divide this unit by the number in the series (8). You get 6. You are earning 6% interest from the debt portion of this hypothetical portfolio.

Now let's look at the equity side of your portfolio. Add the following numbers together: 6 + 7 + 8+ 9+ 10. You get 40. Divide this by the number of items in the series (5). You get 8. The equity side of your portfolio may be evenly divided between five stocks, or groups of stocks, whose dividends are 6%, 7%, 8%, 9%, and 10%. The average dividend yield of this hypothetical portfolio is exactly 8%.

You are striving to meet your income goal. Whether it is 7% or 5% or 3.9%, that percentage is the driver. Set the goal and design to it. The high end of the income range is as much as 7%. You may need less. You will rarely be able to earn more. Even 7% is an ideal. Test yourself against your goal, rather than the number of 7%!

You may wish to think of this as a model. Remember, models are intimations of reality—they are not real. As we discussed in Chapter 3, the model ships and cars and dolls you played with in your youth were toys! They *represented* reality. You understood that as a child. Keep that same understanding today when you design your model portfolio. It is a representative of a real potential.

The hypothetical portfolio above is a half-and-half model. It is simply a way of thinking about the problem of creating retirement income. It is a model of a model; you will design the solution to the problem. There are as many solutions to that problem as there are readers of this book. More than that, actually.

Each solution—your solution—will change with time. As your circumstances change, your portfolio will change. As the economy changes, you will subtly adjust the portfolio to meet those changes. Your income needs may increase for a planned travel event. They will decrease as you mature. Yields from dividends will change. Companies will increase, decrease, or eliminate their dividends. You will move on to other stocks. Bonds will mature and you will replace them by others, with differing interest rates. Inflation and recession will alter your real dollar income needs. Each will alter your portfolio, usually only slightly; occasionally, quite drastically. In any one year the overall portfolio distribution yield may vary between 4% and 7%, at the extremes.

The Folly of Chasing High Yield

A final note before getting into the details. Chasing high yield is a fool's game. Yield is not the driver of these discussions. It is an aspect of them. We are discussing a 7% solution for several reasons. These reasons have nothing to do with trying to achieve the highest possible yield from a portfolio. The 7% figure can be a realistic goal. It is not a necessary goal. It may or may not be a sufficient goal, depending upon your income needs. If your portfolio drives to 5.25%, so be it. If you need 8.3%, you had better consider other choices: more work, more saving, less spending. The portfolio cannot be expected to give it to you. The yield for any investment should be a result of careful consideration of many factors. The net portfolio yield to you may be as high as 7%. If you need less, take less, and allow the remaining to grow for the future. If you need more, seek it elsewhere.

Moderation is the primary characteristic of our design process. Moderation in all things retirement is desirable. We want to be moderate in our selection of the components of the portfolio. The real world gives us a plethora of choices from which to design our portfolio. We may want to grow the portfolio in a manner subsistent to our taking distributions from it.

Often, the simplest solution to a problem is the correct solution. Not always, but enough to make the simple solution worthy of consideration. This principle is called Occam's razor. It is a rule of thumb that is often followed in scientific investigation. Occam's razor suggests that the idea with the fewest assumptions and requirements that answers a question is the correct response.

The simplest solution we can arrive at for portfolio design is 50/50 stocks and bonds. Each side of the equation offers income. The individual bonds offer portfolio stability, as their volatility is much lower than that of stocks. In this portfolio, there is practically no turnover year after year; only if a stock breaks its stop loss or a bond matures do you need to do something. This simple solution is just one of thousands, but it's a place to begin understanding portfolio design.

Recall that we have turned away from the mantra of growth. We have turned to income. Growth still remains important, only less so. Protection is important, too. A portion of the portfolio may be aligned to an investment with either of these goals in mind. That portion becomes of lesser importance. Think of gold or of global small companies or of sovereign debt. Each of these investments can create either growth or risk insurance. They are a far smaller portion of the portfolio in retirement.

A Plethora of Portfolio Designs

Again, there are as many investment approaches to retirement income as there are investors; more, since many change their minds several times in their investing careers. We will try to narrow the range down to those which have come before and have had a reasonable degree of success. You may begin devising your own as you read.

Please know that you are as capable of designing your retirement portfolio as anyone else, provided you are attentive and wise. Rules, formulas, and secret weapons have failed time and again. If you are strong and flexible—like the willow tree or the bamboo—you can thrive in the years to come.

More Basic Arithmetic and Hypothetical Portfolio #2

To demonstrate another approach to portfolio design, consider our hypothetical friends Mr. and Ms. Smith, who are about to retire. Mr. Smith will receive $1,080 and his wife will receive $1,098 from Social Security when they turn 65 next year. A $220 Medicare cost will be deducted from their checks each month, so they will net $1,958. Their Medicare supplemental plan has no monthly premium; they have good health, are non-smokers, and live an active lifestyle.

Mr. and Ms. Smith have gone over their monthly expenses, have agreed upon the figures, and have been able to project that they will need retirement income of $5,250 a month. So far, their income is $1,958, so they are short $3,292. Mr. Smith has saved $178,344 in his 401(k) plan at work. His wife has saved $178,328 in her SEP IRA as a self-employed graphics artist. They each have older IRAs with a total of $34,566. They have $240,000 in the bank, as CDs. Their cash reserves total $40,000. The cash reserves are their emergency/opportunity funds and are not available for income. Thus they have $591,238 as their retirement income source, once they retire. Their first year income from the portfolio will need to be $39,504 ($3,292 x 12).

Now we are ready to begin the design of the Smith's portfolio. They have to have $39,505 income from $591,238. Here's how to figure the yield they will need:

$39,505 x 100 divided by $591,238 = 6.68%

For purposes of simplicity, let's call this 6.7%. Let's put 65% of the portfolio into individual bonds, for the sake of discussion. This leaves 35% to be invested in equities.

Let's construct the bond portfolio first. Sixty-five percent of $591,238 is $384,300:

$591,238 x .65 = $384,300

Thus we have $384,300 to invest in the bond side of the portfolio. As the $200,000 in CDs mature, the Smiths can move them into Build America Bonds (BABs). These are bonds issued by local or state government agencies, a third of whose interest expense is guaranteed by the federal government. They typically have very long maturities, up to 30 years. They are rated. Their yields are a function of time and perceived risk. As of this writing, these yields range from 4.5% to 7.5%, for 5 to 30 years of maturity. The

Smiths will opt for four sets of bonds, yielding 6.5% to 7%. They will have $50,000 increments, ideally spread across 15 to 25 years. The effective net yield will be 6.8%. The annual interest from these bonds will be $13,600 ($200,000 x 6.8 = $13,600).

The remaining $184,300 in the bond side of the portfolio will be portioned out as follows. Keep in mind that these assets are within the Smiths' IRAs. The Smiths will put $14,300 in intermediate term Treasury inflation protected bonds (TIPs). The yield varies each year with inflation. The current yield is 3.2%. Thus, the annual income would be $458. The yield will increase if inflation becomes an economic concern. Thus, if inflation rises to 5%, the yield will rise to 6.85% or $980 that year. The $525 increase in yield is compensation for inflation risk.

The Smiths have $160,000 remaining in the debt portion of their portfolio. What will they do with this amount? There are a variety of investment grade corporate bonds available from firms with excellent credit ratings, low debt, high market penetration for their products or services, and debt coverage ratios over 1.4. The Smiths choose four firms and purchase $40,000 of each of their bonds, with maturities between 5 and 12 years from the purchase date.

As you will recall from Chapter 6, this is called laddering. As each bond matures, the Smiths will search for the best yield and timeline within their risk constraint. During an inflationary time, they may shorten the maturities. They may find that bank CDs offer the best yield. They may also choose to use CDs if the equity portion of the portfolio begins to fall below its stop losses. They can and will switch markets, as well as ladder, when they're feeling cautionary. What they will seek is a yield to match their income goal, rather than the lofty academic goals of diversification, buy and hold, or efficient markets.

The Smiths will purchase their bonds for prices between 98 and 99.85 out of a possible 100. These bonds will pay 6.45% interest as a group. Thus, from the $160,000 portion of their bond portfolio, the Smiths will have $10,370 in annual income. ($160,000 x 6.45% = $10,370.)

Let's look at the total bond portfolio:

Type	Yield	Annual Income	Monthly Income
BABs	6.8%	$13,600	
TIPs	3.2%	$458	
Corporate	6.45%	$10,370	
Total Bonds:	6.3%	$24,400	$2,033
Social Security			$1,958
Total Income			$3,991

The Smiths have $3,991 income from the bond portion of their portfolio plus Social Security. They need $5,250. They must get $1,259 monthly income—or $15,108 annually—from the remaining $206,900 of the portfolio. So:

$$\frac{\$15,108}{\$206,900} = 7.3\%$$

They need to find investments which will net a distribution return of 7.3%.

But there is a catch. Remember that the Smiths put some funds into Treasury inflation protected bonds (TIPs)? They did so as insurance against a rise in inflation. They will do the same on the equity side of their portfolio. Here, they will invest $16,900 into gold—again, as insurance against a significant decline in the value of the dollar and against a significant international event (think terrorist attack).

The Smiths now have $190,000 remaining to invest in their equity portfolio to earn them the $1,259 monthly income. They have to earn 8% from this side of the equation. How can they do such a thing? Isn't this risk personified? Are they crazy to search out such improbable yields? Even if they found these types of yields, would they be sustainable? Could they lose their principal? Where would they begin to look?

The devil is in the detail. If we look diligently enough we can find such yields, offered by firms that are likely to protect our principal. There is a universe of dividend paying stocks with low debt that have been sustaining their distributions for many years. Examples abound both here and in the international arena. Thus, the Smith's portfolio may look like this:

Firm	Investment	Dividend Yield	Annual Income
Firm A	$35,000	7.7%	$2,695
Firm B	$35,000	10.2%	$3,570
Firm C	$35,000	6.8%	$2,380
Firm D	$35,000	9.3%	$3,255
Firm E	$20,000	6.2%	$1,240
Firm F	$30,000	6.8%	$2,025
Total	$190,000	7.98%	$15,165

With an median yield of about 8%, The Smiths have created $1,264 of monthly income from the equity portion of their portfolio ($15,165 divided by 12), a bit more than they need. They've done it; they've reached their income goal. Now their retirement income stream looks like this:

SSI	$1,958
Bonds	$2,033
Equities	$1,264
Total	$5,255

Implementing Your Design

Implementing the portfolio components requires the most technically adept set of skills. Experience is often the best teacher and you may, or may not, have the experience. It cannot be attained solely by research or reading. You must be actively "working the money." This means failing on a regular basis and learning from the mistakes you make. Stop losses are tools to help you make mistakes wisely. There are many computer tools and websites that can be useful in the learning and the implementation process, such as FINVIZ.com, quantumonline.com, dividendinvestor.com, and wikinvest.com. Each website is a learning arena. Each is also a tracking station. Subscribe to them, learn how to use them, and correspond with them on ideas you find useful.

Maintaining the portfolio requires less time and more experience. We'll discuss this in detail in the next chapter. You must maintain the portfolio relative to your income needs and to the market—in that order. Your income needs can increase or decrease, as we have said. Alter the distribution process accordingly. Much of the time the components of the portfolio, once set in place, will perform as expected. They will change in value each day, each week, each month. They will pay out interest and dividends as you have expected. Occasionally, the price will change enough to warrant attention—hopefully with an upward bias!

How to Evaluate Portfolio Elements

How can we evaluate company earnings and the dividends companies pay? Whenever we evaluate, we are making a judgment. These judgments are subjective. While numbers are used extensively, do not be fooled by the use of numbers. The source of the numbers may be accurate—or not so accurate. The interpretation of the numbers may be realistic—but off the mark. The validity of the numbers may be exemplary—or may be a work of fiction.

Forensic accounting is a profitable career for many because any aspect of the accounting record may be manipulated. This means accounting is as much an art as a science. It exhibits qualities of both fields. Manipulation is what an artist does to clay, or to a canvas. It is not bad, except when done by bad people. As Mark Twain famously wrote: "There are three kinds of lies: Lies, damned lies, and statistics."

Forensic accountants are detectives. If they are good at what they do, they can find a variety of needles hidden deeply in haystacks. Justin Fox describes it as "the sausage making involved in economic reports and corporate earnings reports."

Annual reports more often reflect decision based facts than fact based decisions.

Annual reports more often reflect decision based facts than fact based decisions. The demands of quarterly earnings reports to glow fantastical can cause overly optimistic statements. The desires of majority shareholders to pump up net operating income can lead to a variety of income "amplifications." Options exercises can and do drive stock prices—in both directions. Stock buy backs are an easy way to drive up earnings, easier than actually increasing them sometimes. The board makes the decision to take a few million shares out of circulation. Voilà! Earnings per share have increased because the number of shares has declined. They have wasted some capital, but that appears on the cash balance sheet, earnings are on the income sheet. A neat trick, too often employed by large cap firms. If a firm suggests that it is considering options or a buyback scheme for the near future, retire that stallion and look for a better mount. He has gone to pasture.

More Basic Arithmetic and Hypothetical Portfolio #3

As further demonstration of the variety of investment approaches, consider a third hypothetical portfolio, this one belonging to Ms. Johnson, who lost her husband last year and is eager to assure that his life insurance proceeds are well invested to see her through retirement.

Ms. Johnson will design her portfolio from two broad groups, debt and equity. She invests 45% into bonds, 50% into equities, and 5% into TIPS and sovereigns, investments that will insure her against a variety of external risks.

Bonds	$450,000	6.0%	$27,000.00
Stocks	$500,000	8.0%	$40,000.00
TIPS, Sovereigns	$ 50,000	5.5%	$ 2,750.00
Net Yield		7.0%	$69,750.00

The bond group is sorted to yield, quality of debt, length of time to maturity, and price. Ms. Johnson prefers individual bonds and will design a bond ladder with short, intermediate, and long-term durations. She will invest in bonds with staggered maturities of 8 to 14 years, of investment quality (BBB - AAA), and with a yield to maturity (YTM) between 6% and 6.2%, acquired at par or slightly below. She will hold these through their maturity dates. She is not necessarily concerned about their prices as shown on her quarterly statements. She does pay attention to the news about each issuing company. She reads the news and decides whether and how to respond. In virtually all cases, her intention is to wait patiently for the semi-annual deposit of interest into her account. When the bond matures, she will look for a replacement bond. The bond's yield to maturity, duration, quality, and price will be dictated at the time by Mr. Market.

Ms. Johnson has selected the stock group based on an extensive list of criteria: company size, debt-to-equity ratio, price to cash flow, price to book, size, nationality, yield, industry, sector, average trading volume. These are classic, fundamental criteria; see Graham, Buffett, et al. Nothing new here!

There is a dichotomy to the bond and equity investment selection process: Dr. Jekyll and Mr. Hyde. On the one hand, we want bonds that pay reasonable interest relative to the risks we are willing to assume. On the other hand, we want stocks that have low long-term debt-to-equity ratios. Can we be driven by each instinct, the sublime and the base?

Of course we can. We are judging balance sheets with similar standards. Our viewpoint is simply different. We appraise the debt by one group of rules. The firm must be able to service the debt. The debt we are looking for is typically issued by larger, well-regarded firms, with a substantial ability to pay the interest on the debt embedded in the cash flow. The debt cannot be excessive. We define excessive as a more than 70% debt-to-equity ratio.

The equity is appraised in another manner. The equity we are looking for may be from any size firm, but usually from those companies that have few concerns about debt repayment because their debt load is nominal. Dividends should be reasonable, consistent, and growing. Reasonable means they come from net income, rather than from a debt offering. Consistent means they have been made for several years—ideally more than five years. Growing means they are increasing, consistent with free cash flow.

Ms. Johnson will be looking for stocks that have dividend yields between 7% and 10%.

Let's be certain we understand what we mean when we say a stock has a dividend yield. If you buy a stock for $20 a share and that firm has paid $.25 a share dividend over each of the previous four quarters, then it has a dividend yield of 5%:

$$.25 \times 4 = \$1$$

$$\frac{\$1}{\$20} = 5\%$$

Keep in mind that dividend yield is based on history and is not guaranteed in the future. Management retains its control over free cash flow; investors have no say in the matter. Management may decide to do something other than distribute dividends with the company's free cash flow: capital expenditures, share buybacks, acquisitions, debt retirement, and compensation adjustments are but a few of the choices the chief financial officer has on the menu.

It's also worth noting that dividends are usually taxed twice—at the corporate level and at the investor level. While there are many exceptions to this section of the Tax Code (e.g., REITs, LLCs, LPs, and qualified investors), it acts as a drag on the dividend decision. Once dividends begin to be paid out to shareholders, that action does set a precedent and an expectation, but neither is etched into the corporate by-laws. Again, dividends are quarterly decisions made by senior management.

You expect interest payment on corporate debt;
you hope for a continuation of dividend payment on stock.

Now, let's get back to our discussion of Ms. Johnson's portfolio. Again, on the equity side she is looking for stocks that have a dividend yield of 7% to 10%. Let's examine her strategic selection process to see how the math works. This will show you how a combination of securities with a variety of yields can produce the desired result: a 7% yield.

These are examples and are not meant to be representative of what is available to you as you read this book. You will find a nearly infinite number of alternative mixes. This is not meant as a formula, either. Flexibility demands that we discover the best choice for your income need from the current alternatives available. Formulaic designs are to be found elsewhere!

Let's illustrate Ms. Johnson's possible combination:

	Group A	Group B	Group C
1.	6.5%	7.6%	9.5%
2.	6.7%	7.8%	9.8%
3.	7.1%	8.1%	10.1%
4.	7.4%	8.4%	10.8%
5.	7.5%	8.5%	11.1%
Net Yields:	7.04%	8.08%	10.26%

Total Portfolio Net Yield: <u>8.46%</u>

These unnamed but very real examples are from a list of securities meeting the following criteria: debt-to-equity ratio below .7, low price to free cash flow ratio, payout ratio less than 80%, US based, with a dividend yield of 6% or more, from a variety of industries and capitalization sizes. This information is from October 8, 2009 and will change many times before you read this. Research done when you are establishing your portfolio will discover different sets of choices. The choice sets should remain within the range of the parameters we've discussed.

The point here is to demonstrate—from real world examples— how to design the elements of your own portfolio. You may have a choice of large, mid, and small cap firms from several industries and geographical locations, servicing a wide range of markets. With this amalgamation of fifteen securities, justified by the preceding qualifications, you, like Ms. Johnson, can create the equity side of your portfolio.

The Joy of Putting Capital to Work

There is an added dimension to investing that goes beyond meeting your income needs in retirement. It's called the joy of putting capital to work.

Look behind the scenes for just a moment. The companies you will be investing in have had sufficient gross and net income to remain comfortable with distributing dividends to their shareholders. Their products and services continue in high demand. They do not have so much debt on their books that the debt service consumes all of their earnings. They have not chosen to borrow to "juice" their dividends. They retain enough of their net revenue to use for future growth, for employee compensation, for marketing expansion, or for new product or service development. These companies continue to provide jobs—and job security—to their employees. They pay taxes at every conceivable level of government, for a wide variety of legislated hard and soft support. They work within their local communities for the betterment of themselves and their communities' citizens. They can afford a continued social, civic, environmental, cultural, legislative, and political agenda. These agendas provide even more jobs and opportunities within the local and regional geography.

All this and a $1.20 dividend to boot! Ain't capitalism wonderful?

WORKSHEET

Assignment: Build a sample portfolio of stocks and bonds.

Here is where you begin to put the pieces together. Before you actually make the investments, do these research activities and watch a sample portfolio. If you subscribe to FINVIZ.com, you can do back testing, if you so desire.

1. Visit FINVIZ.com and screen from the 55 choices to a short list of stocks that meet your criteria. For example: screen to stocks only (no funds or ETFs), 7% dividend yield, .8 debt to equity, .8 payout ratio, 50,000 average daily trading volume. You can play with these variables as you wish. This is a starting point for portfolio construction.

2. Once you have a list or lists, begin to learn more about each company and each industry or sector. For example, you will want to go into greater depth for BDCs by seeking alpha.com's contributor, Kapitall, or BDCM. The more complex the investment, the more time you want to spend learning and making mistakes.

12

MONITORING AND MAINTAINING YOUR PORTFOLIO

"I'm not so much concerned about a return upon my money as I am about a return of my money."

—Mark Twain quote popularized by Will Rogers

Portfolio monitoring and maintenance are the cornerstones of your retirement income strategy. They are as important as portfolio design and distribution strategies. You neglect the portfolio at your own risk. You should open your statements when they arrive in the mail or email, read them, and react. You react with your mind, your heart, and your emotions: all are valid response devices.

For much of the time, leave well enough alone. Occasionally, you may have to adjust your holdings. Your gut overrules your brain. The facts are less important than the emotions of the time. You change the portfolio. By doing so, you try to protect the value of what you have accumulated. Despite academic sources suggesting otherwise, these alterations can be productive. Rebalancing an income generating portfolio is often counterproductive; making changes every quarter or every year can destroy a portfolio's productivity. It is, however, realistic to stand aside from the turmoil in the economy and step away from the markets when severe conditions warrant it.

You will not always be right. You may find yourself sheepishly returning to the fray after another good economic quarter. Do give yourself permission to react occasionally. All things in moderation. You may alter the investments within your retirement account to reflect the ideas in this book. As with any investment idea, be prepared to change as times change. Also, please remember that the majority is often wrong and is typically entrenched in crowd-like tendencies. With a call or a few keystrokes you can move a portion, or all, of your portfolio to the safe harbor of money markets, bank CDs, or Treasuries.

But What About Transaction Costs?

"But wait!" you say. "What about transaction costs? What impact could they have on the distribution rate of my 7% portfolio?"

As stated in Chapter 5, this type of portfolio tends to have low turnover. Once your investments are in place, they rarely change. Frequent trading occurs elsewhere.

You are only going to sell a stock if it drops below your 10% stop loss. Your equities will have more volatility than your bonds. You will pay acquisition and disposal costs. Over seven years, with 15 stocks in the portfolio, you can reasonably expect up to three to break through their stop loss each year. At that point you sell the stock and replace it with something more promising. Over a seven-year time horizon, you can expect transaction costs for equities to be about as low as the least costly fund or ETF.

> **You are only going to sell a stock if it drops below your 10% stop loss.**

On the debt side of your portfolio, as each bond matures, you will replace it. With eight bonds of laddered maturities over eight years, you will buy a bond once a year. Acquiring each bond will have a cost. There is no cost to redeem the bond at maturity.

For example, your intermediate bond portfolio may have a duration of five to ten years. These are investment grade bonds with a nominal chance of default risk across the entire economic cycle. Thus, there is a low probability of your buying or selling within the bond portfolio during this time. If, historically, 2.5% of these bonds default, your risk is quite small. The average of this 5- to 10-year timeline is 7.5 years. We can assume that the costs are spread out over seven years for each bond. The net cost to run the bond portfolio is .14% each year. This compares more than favorably to the lowest priced bond funds on the market.

Enjoy Growth, But Reduce Risk
as Retirement Approaches

Growth is a secondary objective in asset management. Holding on to a security may lead to its appreciation in value. If that occurs, then you may be delighted to find the stock appreciate in price over time. You might consider this growth as a negative cost!

As an example, buying stock during 2009 was a turkey shoot. Virtually anything and everything went up in price. Look at the preferreds. From June 2008 through March 2009 they dropped by 50% in aggregate price. There were few instances, outside of the financials, where the drop in price was underpinned by reason. Fear had taken hold. No one wanted to buy; everyone wanted to sell. This led to the aberration of 50%+ discounts in the preferred, non-financial marketplace. Acquiring a select number of these preferreds led to you earning 10% to 16% on the capital invested. By the spring of 2009 you could buy any number of preferred stocks—again, outside of the financials—with yields two to three times normal, at prices less than half of just nine months earlier. Recall Baron Rothschild's comment in 1874, as the streets around the Paris Bourse were riotous from the Communard revolution: "Buy when blood runs in the street." It does take nerve to walk into a theatre from which everyone else is running. You often get the best seat in the house. Model your actions after Warren Buffet: "I buy when everyone else is selling; I sell when everyone else is buying."

Price aberrations do not last long in the market. These preferred stocks are now trading back at typical prices of $24 to $26 a share. Had you purchased these stocks during the late spring of 2009, your rates of return with this capital would now be in the low teens. This occurred with no underlying change in the value of the security. You would have fattened up the yields within your stock portfolio considerably with these acquisitions. If you had sat out most of the year and bought back into the markets during the summer of 2009, your acquisition cost would still have been much lower, your yield on this portion of your portfolio would still be in the low teens, and you would be sleeping well at night—both during and after the market collapse.

These opportunities happen during economic crises. Look to these times as ideal retirement dates. If you find yourself about to retire, you should be repositioning your 401(k) or IRA accounts more conservatively as the date approaches. Why risk losing during the last months of your career what decades of slow accumulation have created?

Having reduced the risk in your portfolio as you approach your retirement, you can dedicate yourself to other aspects of preparation. This new life ahead will require serious attention to health benefits, available or absent, for you during retirement. You may wish to use accumulated sick pay or vacation pay to finally pay off the balance on your home mortgage. Extending certain benefits available from your employer may be your choice. You may be selling the business, or a rental. Put the retirement accounts on hold in a money market for the final months of your career and spend the time on other pursuits.

Once you have retired, you will roll the 401(k) or 403(b) into your IRA and consolidate your retirement funds—in a money market. If you are so lucky as to have retired at the height of a recession, or even if you have been laid off, look happily to your future! This new retirement venture will be the next step in your life. Walk forward knowing that risk has been removed from your portfolio.

While all about you is desperation and trouble, you are gainfully unemployed and loving it. Why the joy? You have been wise (and lucky) enough to have saved your portfolio from ruin and you are now able to buy as blood runs in the Street!

The Impact of the Economy on Your Lifestyle

How will the economy change your lifestyle during retirement? Each year the answer to this question will change. During boom years—and most of the time the economy does well—you will pay far more attention to your lifestyle than to your assets. Your portfolio will grow at some reasonable rate, your income will also grow, and you will pay less attention to the internal workings of the market beast.

In lean times, you may see your assets shrink in value. You will pay closer attention. Bonds will continue reasonably well, while you may have to walk away from more and more stocks. When the economy goes into recession, we all tighten our belts, almost naturally. Others don't spend, so we tend to do the same.

We are all members of tribes. We do work and play together; we do follow leaders and trends. Thus, fewer shoppers may prompt others to shop less, until equilibrium is reached. Firms that have sold down their inventories have to rebuild them in response to growing demand, and stock prices will reverse course. The shopping begins again—we always have to provide for our families.

During a recession, you may find that you reduce your family expenses to reflect changing economic conditions. You recall Joseph in Egypt. Saving for the lean times during the good times has always proven to be an excellent investment strategy!

During times of inflation, expenses will rise. Your income from Social Security will also rise, as may your pension and your rents, if you own rental property. Your portfolio may also see an increase in distribution. Firms do well as prices rise. They may raise their prices. They may increase their profitability. This can result in an increase in free cash flow, an increase in net income, and an increase in dividends paid to shareholders. They may also have to renegotiate their debt, forcing up the yields on their bonds, which you may be buying each year to replace those maturing within your portfolio. Inflation, the scourge of monetary policy gone amok, may be the portfolio's good friend. Yes, your cost of living will increase; ideally, so will your income stream.

The Impact of Non-Natural Events on Your Portfolio

News will come out that affects aspects of your portfolio, or all of it. In early 2010, many retirees in the UK and the US owned shares in BP. The company was cash rich, had virtually no debt, had massive free cash flow, and paid a mighty dividend. It was the ideal candidate for the value investor seeking retirement income. It happened to possess all the characteristics of the value stock that we find of interest. Out of the blue, two events concurred to rain terror on the shareholders. First came the Macondo rig explosion in the Gulf of Mexico in April 2010. The stock price plummeted but the dividend remained untouched.

Had you been invested, share prices would have fallen through your stop loss, certainly. Should you have bought back in at the half-price sale?

Next, the US government fined BP $20.1 billion and forced a suspension of its dividend. The price actually stabilized on the announcement of the fine. Investors wondered: Do I buy back in or add to my holdings? What about the bonds? They were AA+ rated until Fitch, Moody's, and Standard & Poor's lowered BP's debt rating to AA in response to the disaster. If you re-examine BP's financials, $22 billion in annual free cash flow should have carried any projected liability cost. Government intervention is a fixed fight. You have to review your holdings.

Actually, buying the BP bonds maturing in two years offered a massive yield-to-maturity of 7% to 8% for a very short duration risk. Bill Gross at PIMCO bought $100 million in just a few days. Look at the streets, don't listen to the Street. Red is your friend. Leave your sentiment at the door of your retirement portfolio. You must be as cold and as calculating as those Big Boys who run multi-billion dollar hedge funds. An amoral response to asymmetric opportunity is as good a bet as you can make in the market. Very simple. You have to have the courage to support your lifestyle. If this fight is too big for you, or one you'd rather ignore, then do so. There are many ways to earn your portfolio income. Sell and walk away. Choose your play. You are paying!

With some frequency, economic change—recession or inflation—will hit the global economy. You must adjust your portfolio to meet these new assumptions.

As we've discussed, inflation can erode the value of your bonds. But you have trained yourself to buy a bond and hold it until it is redeemed. You have staggered the bonds over time to manage duration risk. You will usually hold these bonds to maturity, as their price will slowly move to $100 with the approach of the maturity date. The negative impact of inflation on the bond ladder, while increasingly obvious with rising inflation, will not affect your investment if the bond matures. Remember, you have tried to pay less than $100 for each bond and you will receive $100 at maturity. The change in value during the holding period is immaterial to you. When the bond matures, you will look to buy from the market a bond with a higher yield. This increases your income. You will buy it, hopefully at a discount to par, earn the higher coupon, and hold it to maturity. This increase in yield ideally will give you more income to match your rising cost of living.

Protecting your portfolio against the impact of recession brings us to our next subject, risk management.

Protecting Your Assets from Risk

When an economic crisis hits, how do you protect your assets from risk? We may better ask: How do you manage the risks inherent in your 7% portfolio?

Let's go back to the hypothetical stock portfolio we designed for Ms. Johnson in Chapter 11.

Ms. Johnson's General Portfolio

Bonds	$450,000	6.0%	$27,000.00
Stocks	$500,000	8.0%	$40,000.00
TIPS, Sovereigns	$ 50,000	5.5%	$ 2,750.00
Total	$1,000,000		
Total Portfolio Net Yield:		7.0%	$69,750.00

Ms. Johnson's Stock Portfolio

	Group A	Group B	Group C
1.	6.5%	7.6%	9.5%
2.	6.7%	7.8%	9.8%
3.	7.1%	8.1%	10.1%
4.	7.4%	8.4%	10.8%
5.	7.5%	8.5%	11.1%
Net Yields:	7.04%	8.08%	10.26%

Total Stock Portfolio Net Yield: <u>8.46%</u>

First, the selection criteria weeds out higher risk securities. These criteria eliminate US and global companies with high debt and low cash flow. Like Ms. Johnson, we have little interest in highly leveraged companies. We are interested in value firms. We want stocks that pay a dividend. We also know, from Dr. Seigel, that dividend paying stocks have consistently returned better than non-dividend paying stocks.

Second, each of the individual stocks represents an investment of about $33,333 (assuming an equal distribution across the field of 15 stocks). Each stock represents less than 4% of the portfolio. Ms. Johnson has diversified by means of debt to equity, price to book, historically sustainable dividends, and corporate flexible capital expenditure.

Third, each stock carries an initial 10% stop loss. If the stock declines in price by more than 10% of the original purchase price, Ms. Johnson sells the stock. She walks away, saying to herself, "My bad." She looks forward. She accepts the loss as a lesson. She knows and expects these losses to occur and knows there will be many more opportunities to choose. So should you.

Fourth, the defensive elements in the portfolio—TIPS, sovereign debt, and gold—may provide Ms. Johnson with some global stability. She expects only to pay an insurance premium from this aspect of the equation. Recall that it is only 5% of her total portfolio. Its function is to defend against worst case scenarios, such as the fall and winter of 2008 and 2009, the currency crisis of 1997, or 9/11. Unexpected events such as 9/11 result in losses to the portfolio. They are the price we pay to take risk, to earn better income. We try to insure the risk with these positions. Each of them may insure against a specific risk. All of them work independently.

Your portfolio insurance is the stop loss. In a cascading market, you will first receive notice of the stop loss. You will next have to decide what to do upon the notice. You will then have to make the trade. You have to know that you may lose more than the 10% of your trigger in a systemically illiquid market. The stop loss enables you to attempt to limit your total portfolio risk to 5% (10% of 50% of the portfolio). In 2000 and again in 2008, you would have had the real time experience of 8% to 12% losses. While a heavy blow, you stand tall compared to the "buy and hold" folks. Ask them to show you their year-end statement from either of those years. Show them yours. Console them. Move on.

The bond side of Ms. Johnson's portfolio may reflect some decline in value as well. Her concern here is less on the current value of the bonds than on the stability, strength, and survivability of the issuing company. If she has undertaken her due diligence wisely, she will hold each bond to maturity. Price volatility here is typically lower than in the equity markets. Precipitous declines can occur, however, as was the case with GM bonds in 2008, when politics overrode 300 years of corporate law. *Caveat emptor.*

Managing risk means thinking again about portfolio truths we have been taught since the 1960s. For example, let's discuss the idea of buy and hold and its corollary, holding period risk. How does this manage risk? Practitioners say that, over time, your risk of losing money in the stock market declines. They observe this risk is nearly zero over 20-year time lines and longer. They further state that your rate of return will be greater the longer you hold your position. It will approach the rate of return of the market itself. Buy and forget becomes the mantra. Just keep giving us money and we will do our best for you. If you are fully invested, you can ignore the challenges of market entry and exit. You can forget about transaction costs and tax consequences. The holding period determines the return. Quite simple. Now move along. Ignore the bodies falling from the sky.

This is certainly true when the markets are in a general upward climb. But it ignores the constantly invisible yet ever present fact of current risk. Current risk is the risk of portfolio loss—getting hammered, wiped out—immediately, without warning, and precipitously during the next crisis. It also ignores the fact that:

The longer you are investing on a regular basis (think 401-k), the more you have at risk and the more you have to lose.

These risks are entirely different from holding period risk.

Current risk means that the longer you are invested, the more often you participate in market declines. Size risk means that the more you have invested, the more you have to lose. You need to be aware of these risks. You and your advisor need to have a method of dealing with these risks. Stock and bond ratings, risk assessment tools and models like efficient market theory do not deal with these risks. They ignore them.

Using the Stop Loss to Assist in Decision Making

Your stop loss is your friend. Honor it. Use it for the purpose it was intended. That purpose is to remove as much emotion from your decision making as possible.

Understand that rational thought can lead to irrational action.

> **Your stop loss is your friend. Honor it.**

Under pressure, fight or flight takes control. Respect these. The signals your brain receives or sends may or may not be correct. Logic can work wonders in many ways. Rational behavior and rational models are quite good, quite often. When they fail, you lose. Faulty logic can destroy trillions in wealth in a remarkably short period of time. Consider the complex emotional responses we have to the changes in our wealth. Our portfolio statement value goes down—how do we respond?

There is an action—a logical action—that can remove or at least greatly reduce the element of risk. The action is the stop loss. If a security declines in value by a predetermined amount, we have already made the decision to sell. We have not removed the irrational response to the behavior of the marketplace from our brainstem—we have forced ourselves to respect it and use the force to our advantage. The Chinese have understood this for a very long time. It is called Tai Quon Dao—the ballet of battle, formalized into the slow dance of healthful balance. Try it. Your portfolio will be glad you did.

There is more to the stop loss than acting as a simple prophylactic. In addition to preventing further loss, it can also protect the life of the portfolio. It may be better to protect the life of the womb than the life in the womb. Wedded to a position, you can lose your portfolio's life—and your lifestyle. Learn to just say no. Walk away.

As the prices of the stocks move up, you may consider moving the stop loss points with them. Let's use an example. If you buy a 6% dividend paying stock at $20 a share, your stop loss is $2 (because 10% of $20 is $2). If the price declines to $18, you sell, walk away, lick your wounds, and learn the lesson. It happens.

If the price moves up to $30 (certainly would be nice to see that!), you change the stop loss to $27. If the price drops below $27, you sell out—at a profit of $7, or 35%.

You have been earning the dividend, too. If you have held the stock for a year and it pays the dividend of 6%, you have received an additional $1.20. You have made $8.20 over the one-year holding period, or 41%.

This is a gross return. You have to net it for transaction costs and taxes. You will have to pay tax upon the gain and the dividend, if it is in a non-qualified account. Let's assume a commission of 1% and a combined tax of 25%. For this discussion the commission would be $.40 and the tax would be an additional $1.75. The "transaction cost" of $2.15 is debited from your gross profit of $7 and you get to keep $4.85. You have retained a net profit of 24.3% ($4.85 divided by $20.00).

Take these figures to the real portfolio world. If you have invested $33,000 and earned a net profit of 24.3%, you have created wealth for yourself of $8,019. If you have done this within a qualified account, like an IRA, then you have a net profit of $9,649.

When you take the income from the qualified account, you will pay taxes upon that income at your current tax bracket.

Of course, if you continue to hold, to earn the dividend when paid, you monitor the price. Own a stock long enough and you could very well recover your entire cost basis simply from dividends. Your income will be enviable.

A $20 investment earning a 5% dividend yield will recover its cost in 20 years through dividends alone. Cost recovery is the ultimate joy of dividend investment. If the stock appreciates in value over the years, you may double the impact of your wise investing: once from dividends, again from appreciation.

Monitoring the Elements of Your Portfolio

Attention needs to be paid to the details of your portfolio. Details can be your friend and ally. Should you ignore them, they can turn on you. As facts change, offer yourself the choice of changing your mind.

You want to know about each company's financials and the dividend opportunities that lie within. You must want to follow the firms, their news, their financials, their competitors, and their products.

How to do this? It would take Benjamin Graham months of digging to find the facts in the 1940s. It would cost a mutual fund or hedge fund the annual salaries of an assortment of CFAs to do a thorough job. Of course, they pass that cost on to you. As there are so many of you investing in the funds, the cost is spread out so that you don't even feel the prick of the needle. This is the needle that they insert into your portfolio and drain it of life blood—the annual management fee.

Today, if you have the moxie, you can do a significant portion of this research yourself. Your access to data is now virtually the same as theirs. Your trading costs are the same or less. All of the other costs of ownership, as we discussed earlier, are avoided in your own portfolio. Style drift, portfolio turnover, lack of transparency, management changes, trading costs, distribution fees, many commissions, and marketing charges all disappear when you manage your own portfolio.

In exchange, you have to do the work. It is far less work than the CFAs have to do, as you have a smaller, trackable, easy to understand, personal portfolio that you have made the effort to design and track.

How do you track it? Go online and introduce yourself to either of these free or voluntary subscription websites:

divideninvestor.com

quantumonline.com

FINVIZ.com

wikinvest.org

alpha.com

yahoo.com

Spend some time understanding their mechanics. Just play on the field. Save each site for reference and research. Read their instructions and apply them to your own ideas.

For example, let's examine FINVIZ.com. Here you can pick from an enormous (55) assortment of stock parameters. If you follow the ideas here, then sort the universe of stocks they follow (6,800+) to those with 7%+ dividends, D/E less than .8, and strong free cash flow. You can sort to the US or international. You will discover a range of stocks. Depending upon when you start this, you may find a mixture of MLPs, REITs, a few bank and insurance firms, some oil and gas companies, a few tech firms, mortgage companies—even a few consumer staples and cyclical stocks.

Now go to dividendinvestor.com. Register, pay their subscription, and perform a sort of dividend paying stocks here. The process is different, but the instructions are simple. Here you will have created a list of dividend paying stocks similar to your FINVIZ list, but you can now sort to length of time dividends have been paid—dividend sustainability.

Now move over to quantumonline, pay the voluntary subscription (a one man shop in Montana and quite a nice guy!), and learn more detail about the firms that interest you. Learn here also, in far greater detail than these pages will allow, the mechanics of MLPs, REITs, preferreds, and the like.

If you have a technical bent, try wikinvest. Here, you can design tracking tools and listen to other opinions for your stocks (recall that they are opinions, nothing more. Yours is more valid: it is your money, rather than theirs!

You can create your own lists of securities at each of these sites. The interplay between these is your contribution to the success of your portfolio. Edgar, FINRA, NASDAQ, NYSE: each of these sites will offer you extremely in-depth information on the financials of all stocks. As you enter these realms, you enter the den of dragons. Here the raw financial information from a company is in full view. You will have to be able to sort through it, to know how and when firms are lying or obfuscating, and to know the bent of the regulators' perspectives. While deeply immersed in facts and legalities, these sites are also entirely works of art. Paint by numbers reigns supreme. Despite the volume of data, this is where Enron, Global Crossing, LTCM, Bernie Madoff, and the regulators "make play in the fields of the Lord."

Herein lie monsters, as the charts from the 16th century proclaimed, at the borders of the known world. Just know that the adventure of economics, econometrics, and data mining begins at the margins. Know too that the smallest boats have navigated the deepest oceans. Columbus and Magellan's yachts held no advantage over today's bareboat Caribbean charter, yet discovered the New World, the globe itself. Your entry here is to discover more, as you are impelled to do so.

You can make effective decisions at the level of the websites first listed. You can work there to design and maintain your comfortable retirement portfolio. The tools you bring to the market before you shop—selectivity, stop loss, sizing, insurance—are of primary importance. Use them. Answer the door each day that Mr. Market calls with your own response. Silence is very often the very best policy.

Once you have chosen your stocks, leave the remainder in the stable. You can easily create tracking lists on each site. When you fail with a stock, replace it with another from the stable. Constantly revisit and replenish the stable with fresh stock. The members will change with time. Only a few stay on the list. Most appreciate off your list, as their value is taken up, along with the price, by others. The data feeds to each website are slightly "seasoned"—that is, old. Rely upon all of the websites together, rather than simply one. They may update daily, weekly, monthly, or quarterly. Follow the news reports, as listed on each stock's FINVIZ or Yahoo! page.

Once you have made a decision, pay attention to the price you pay for each position. The stop loss defines the automatic alarm.

As an example of monitoring risk in a bond portfolio, consider GM senior debt in 2008. Those bonds would have lost nearly their entire value if their owners held through the winter and the federal government takeover. If you were paying attention during the fall, you saw the news daily. You read each report on GM. As the bonds dropped below the 10% stop loss, you would have had to make a decision to hold onto them or sell them. It was a tough call. GM had been the backbone of American manufacturing for a century. Few expected them to fail; fewer still expected the bondholders to fail, even in bankruptcy. Three hundred years of contract law protected each holder of senior debt in the company. You may well have held the bond, waiting patiently for maturity or for the bankruptcy court to pay out the bondholders' claims. When the federal government negotiated the settlement in the late winter, the bondholders were left with less than 15% of their position, and that in the form of newly issued stock. Politics trumped law.

Monitoring stocks involves more than simply watching the ticker price. Remember that when a dividend is paid, the price of the stock declines by the dividend amount. If you happen to have bought the stock a few weeks prior to the ex-div (the date when the dividend is paid out) date and, for whatever reason, the price declined toward your stop loss, the dividend could drop the stock price below the stop loss. In this event, you may want to adjust your stop loss to reflect the dividend.

Sometimes a change in the price of a security can reflect that institutional traders, hedge funds, or insiders expect a change in dividend. For example, if the company becomes part of an index, that may drive its price, if only temporarily. Institutional investors have to rebalance their portfolios to include the new listing and exclude its replacement. Pay attention to the news on the company. If a dividend payment is terminated, the price of the stock may rise. The market may feel the decision was appropriate and reward it with a positive price change.

Barclays Bank is a case in point. Its stock price had declined precipitously, along with virtually all other financial stocks in the fall and winter of 2008 and 2009. In February of 2009, the Bank of England unilaterally decided that all UK banks would have to stop paying dividends, given the financial morass that the world peered into during that desperate winter. Barclays sold its I Shares unit to Black Rock for $1.2 trillion in 2009. The price of the stock dropped no further and rose significantly thereafter.

You never know. Advisors at every level also never know. Logical responses are often the least useful means of accomplishing your financial goals; they are but one of several response choices. To paraphrase a Chinese quan, you may "sit quietly, doing nothing." Being afraid and walking away from a portion, or all, of a portfolio is another response. Only your own experience—and courage—will determine how you choose to react to financial events. Buy and hold, while more often than not a good investment strategy, should be an approach taken only during the best of times. Keep in mind that since 1999, the S&P 500 index has shown virtually no growth at all—it trades at essentially the same price today as it did then, excluding reinvested dividends. Only by including reinvested dividends does it show any growth at all. Investing, like economics, is not a science. Remember, this is your money, your retirement.

The logical response to the Barclays dividend suspension would have been to sell the stock and look for another. Certainly the wisdom of the times held that any equity was foolish, as capitalism was supposedly self-destructing before our eyes. The report of its demise was widely disseminated—and wrong again.

Make your own decisions. The crowd is far more often wrong than right, especially on Wall Street!

The Power of Flexibility

Flexibility is your defense. Think of water dripping onto a rock—a hard basaltic rock. The water hits the surface, runs down the side, and disappears. The rock is strong, firm, unaffected. What happens over time? The dripping becomes a steady erosive stream of a corrosive molecule (H_2O). The firmness of the rock becomes its weakness. A small crater forms. It erodes into a crevice. The water runs into the opening and splits the rock. Given enough time, the rock will become stones, then pebbles, and finally dust. The flexibility of water conquers the firmness of rock!

If you have ever been to a glacial field, you have seen this at work. The glacier calves in the near distance, growling in its thrust against the river valley. The iridescent new ice is a deep ocean blue. The rocks just ahead of the glacier path are scarred from its crushing presence. As you step further away from the ice wall, the rocks begin to take on a subtle sheen. It is the first growth of algae moss. The moss is living off the nutrients from the rock surface. Step away again and you see rocks covered with moss, with sprouts of young plants emerging from the thickening growth. A hundred meters more and the rocks are stones. Bushes and trees abound in the new tiny forest. The river, flush with the cold glacial runoff, feeds the forest. Flexible life forms and water dominate the rocky valley floor.

Flexibility in the design, structure, and maintenance of your portfolio can keep it strong and vital.

Replacing Portfolio Elements

When your stop loss triggers a sale and you need to replace elements of your portfolio, bear in mind the income you will need. That income can be at any rate of distribution: 4%, 5%, 6%, or 7%. The rate of distribution is in direct response to your need for retirement income. The lower your portfolio yield, the easier achieving that yield becomes and the more conservative your design will be. Always remembering our flexibility code: we can create a "muster list" of available securities from which we may draw our regiment. We have artillery (bonds) and we have foot soldiers (stocks).

The artillery should be designed to last for the duration, to be free from attack, and to have long range fire power. We want a net distributed yield of 6% for the entire bond portfolio. We want that yield ideally from from BBB to AAA investment or institutional grade debt that we purchase at face value or below.

We will hold the bonds to maturity. We will adjust the duration to reflect our opinion of current market conditions. It may vary from two years to twelve years, or more. We'd like the bond yield to be above the firm's dividend yield, if the firm pays a dividend. If that bond yield is lower, we may consider the dividend—for tax purposes, if appropriate. As one piece of field armament runs low on munitions (matures) we will replace that resource with another field piece (buy another bond). Emma. org, Investinginbonds.com, and FINRA.org will be our information resources. Should a piece misfire (stop paying interest), we will replace it immediately.

There are a variety of foot soldiers available. Their skill, weapons, experience, ability, and type are important to our tactical approach. Use the acronym SWEAT to recall these. Skill is dividend paying ability. Weapons are the dividends themselves. Experience is the history of dividend paying. Ability is their low debt claims against gross income. Type is the sector or industry which the firm represents. In the parlance of asset allocation, we may choose from large, mid, and small capitalized firms. Our intent is to focus on distributed earnings. Asset allocation is of less importance to us than income sourcing.

In fact, there are several fine dividend paying firms in each category. Large cap firms may include Reynolds American, AT&T, and Duke Energy: each have paid more than 6%, with little debt and a long history of dividend payments. Midcap firms might include Realty Income, Century Tel, and Cincinnati Financial, all meeting the same criteria. Small caps might be Dorchester Minerals, Terra Nitrogen, and Zenith National. Here are nine stocks that have been paying significant, increasing dividends for many years and that have little long-term debt on their books. This is not a recommendation to invest in these stocks. You have to make the call—a call relative to your income need, your risk tolerance, your tax situation, and your experience. You could, nevertheless, do worse in a growth portfolio—and have little or no income to show for your efforts.

Choose to ignore the high flyers, hot stocks, and best managed fund of the year in favor of consistent returns based upon sound investing. Noise in the marketplace is interesting, but tells you little or nothing about your portfolio. Ignore it. Make your own pathway, or use a financial advisor who doesn't follow the crowd. Remember, the crowd is far more often wrong than correct.

How Income Is Paid from Your Portfolio to You

What is the mechanism by which you actually receive income from your portfolio? Bonds pay their interest every six months. Stocks pay their dividends every three months.

Your portfolio will have a few thousand dollars in a money market account. This account will act as the conduit to receive your interest and dividend distributions. It will make a monthly electronic distribution to your local checking account, the one you use to pay bills and draw upon for everyday expenses. The cash flow from your portfolio into the money market account will be done automatically. Your Social Security check will be directly deposited into your local checking account, as well.

By monitoring and maintaining your portfolio—replacing new crops when old ones mature or succumb to inclement weather—you will receive the income you need. You plant according to your needs, in rhythm with the season. You do not chase yield—you harvest it.

WORKSHEET

Assignment: Establish a monitoring program with your brokerage firm.

Now you are going to put your money where your ideas are. You have the stock pieces, you have the bonds. Invest. Monitor. Relax.

1. Establish and respond to stop losses.

2. Set up notices of bond maturities.

3. Establish an annual report showing monthly dividend and interest payments within your accounts.

13

THE TAXMAN COMETH

Put not your trust in money, but put your money in trust.
—Oliver Wendell Holmes

Taxes are the bane of every citizen of the Republic. Judge Learned Hand, Justice of the US Court of Appeals earlier in the twentieth century, said:

"Anyone may arrange his affairs so that his taxes shall be as low as possible; he is not bound to choose that pattern that best pays the treasury. There is not even a patriotic duty to increase one's taxes. Over and over again, the courts have said that there is nothing sinister in so arranging affairs as to keep taxes as low as possible. Everyone does it, rich and poor alike, and all do right, for nobody owes any public duty to pay more than the law demands."[1]

You should take seriously your responsibility to reduce your tax burden to the lowest level legally possible, each and every year. By doing so, you manage your retirement income far more effectively than managing it to a particular yield, such as 7%.

Your income objective during retirement should be to maintain the lowest possible tax bracket, year in, year out. View tax bracket management as a game. The rules change each year, the figures you play with change, even the players change; yet it is a game you can win—quite easily, actually. Learn the rules that apply to you. Spend some time each year updating your knowledge. If you have committed to managing the portfolio wisely, you are committed to a few hours a week already. Add a few hours at the end of each year, in preparation for the following year. It is your money, your time, your retirement. Spend each wisely.

> **Your income objective during retirement should be to maintain the lowest possible tax bracket.**

Taxes and Your Portfolio

Your portfolio during retirement can significantly contribute to this reduction process. Where individual investments are held is important. Your understanding of the taxation of earnings is critical. Working the Tax Code to your advantage is imperative to keeping more income for yourself. That means understanding tax brackets and your marginal tax rate, and working that information to your advantage. The tax advisor with whom you work must have the competence and the interest to keep up with you and with the Code. You should view the sum you pay your tax advisor as a worthy price to pay for professional advice received.

Federal legislation is often exploited for the betterment of senior management. Regulatory dictate can open doors to fiscal exploitation: the carry trade of recent years provided wide gates of interest rate differential between currencies to drive truckloads of capital through—and out of—the nation. Taxes are simply another form of regulatory dictate. They are grossly unfair and thus fully exploitable by powered interests. They are also exploitable by you. The Tax Code is an ever-changing landscape. It is a canvas upon which you paint by numbers. Where you place the numbers is important.

Where to Hold: Taxable or Tax-Deferred?

Generally, you have two choices in which to hold your investments: taxable (non-qualified) accounts or tax-deferred (qualified) accounts. A taxable (non-qualified) account is one held in your name, jointly with your spouse or family member, or in the name of your trust.[2]

Corporate bonds belong in tax-deferred retirement accounts. Why? The interest they pay you is taxable as ordinary income, so defer it.

Municipals belong in taxable accounts, as they are tax free, at least at the national level. Dividends belong in taxable accounts. Why? Because you can exploit the bracketing differential. They are taxed at lower rates than ordinary income.

Gold and silver ETFs belong in the tax-deferred account. Any change in value does not receive the benefit of capital gains treatment. So too with exchange traded notes (ETNs), the currency and commodity ETF variations.

MLPs should be held in taxable accounts to receive full advantage of the preferential treatment of their distributions. It will also make your CPA happy, as he will get extra compensation for reading the K-1s and tracking cost basis for you year after year. MLPs may be held in a tax-deferred account, however, provided the sum is less than $1 million or so, as this can trigger unrelated business tax income (UBTI).

BDCs are the most complex instruments you may employ in your arsenal. They generate significant amounts of capital gain (and loss), ordinary income, and dividends. They are typically suited for the tax-deferred account.

Immediate annuities are best used outside of the tax-deferred account, as a portion of the distribution is a return of invested principal and therefore tax free. There is much discussion about fixed or variable annuities held within a tax deferred account or a taxable one. If the latter, any capital gains or dividends received are treated as ordinary income; if in the former, you are using a tax-deferred vehicle within a tax-deferred account. Both points are correct. Your call.

REITs issue a K-1 each March, again a favorite for your CPA—more work, more fees. Depreciation is the primary culprit—in a taxable account it must be tracked. Thus, it can be reasonably argued that REITs are better suited for the tax-deferred account. Income from the more unusual sources you may have should be discussed with your CPA prior to investing.

At a personal level, the dual impacts of regulation and taxation can have a devastating effect upon your wealth. The more you know about purported changes before they are enacted, the better prepared you will be. Your tax and financial advisors should be giving you details before the enactment of rule or tax changes, not after. A summer meeting with both, during their downtimes, can be extremely valuable.

Tax-Wise Withdrawal of Portfolio Income

The rules of the tax road will affect how you draw upon your portfolio income. For example, after age 59-1/2 but before your reach the age of 70-1/2, you may take from your qualified account (IRA, etc.) what you wish, what you need. No later than the year after that point, you *must* take from the qualified accounts. The process is dictated by either of two tables from the IRS. Each year you will have to take more than the year before. This portfolio income may or may not be necessary for your lifestyle—but it is necessary for the IRS. They want the taxes—deferred until this time—on the capital, and they want more each year.

There are so many ways to skin the tax cat, even when you must pay the tax. Here, you could make a gift of a portion of the IRA—up to $100,000 each year. You can use the amount gifted as your required minimum distribution (RMD). You can make a donation to a charity each year, the deduction for which dampens or eliminates the taxes due upon the IRA distribution.

Alternatively, you may consider a Roth conversion. This rarely works for someone over 45 to 50 with more than $100,000 in an IRA, but if you are young enough and have a small enough IRA, consider it. You convert the IRA to a Roth IRA, pay the taxes due upon the converted amount from another source of capital, and the new Roth is now free from taxation, forever.[3]

Factoring Taxes in Your Non-Qualified Account Yields

When selecting investments outside your 401(k), IRA, or Keogh, remember to factor taxes into the total return. Taxes are due upon any gain that is realized and recognized in a non-qualified account, according to the Internal Revenue Service. Securities are purchased at a price. Later, that security is sold. If the difference between these two prices is positive, then taxes are due. If the holding period for the security is more than twelve months, the gain is taxed at the current long-term capital gains rate. If it was held for less than the requisite twelve months, the gain is taxed at the short-term capital gains rate. The short-term rate is the same as the rate you pay on ordinary income, such as W-2 income.

This is why it can make sense to invest in tax-free municipals. For example, suppose you invested $10,000 into a tax-free municipal bond yielding 4% and another $10,000 into a taxable bond yielding 5.5%. While the higher yielding bond looks more attractive on the surface, if you are in the 33% bracket, after taxes you will receive $400 for from the municipal bond but only $368.50 from the taxable bond. What the taxable bond would have to yield to give you the same return as the municipal bond is called the *taxable equivalent yield*.

The Power of Tax-Deferred Accumulating

Those who have not yet begun to save for retirement have a world of opportunity ahead. This act of saving is a decision that, once made, becomes automatic. The immediate effects are real; the long-term effects are enormous. Follow this example—and act upon it! This is the most powerful tool you have. Give yourself but one choice here: use this tool! Ignore anyone who says otherwise, ignore yourself if you say, "I'll start next month." Whatever your age, this is the most important lesson in your financial career.

The First Lesson: The Power of Saving. Let's assume that you are 30 and that you have a decent job where you earn $30,000 a year. The firm where you work offers a 401(k) plan. The plan allows you to defer a portion of your current income. The firm matches half of the first 6%, or 3%, of salary that you defer.

By deferring the income, you do not pay taxes today on that amount. For the sake of illustration, let's look at the result of your deferring $1,800 a year, or 6% of your income. The firm gives you an additional $900 (half of $1,800). So you now have $2,700.

You do not pay taxes on the $1,800 you defer. If you are in the 15% federal tax bracket and a 3% state tax bracket, you save $324 in taxes not paid. If you did not defer the $1,800 into the plan, your net take-home on that amount would be $1,476. So to be in the plan, your out-of-pocket cost (what you would have taken home if you did not participate) is $1,476. But wait—by being in the 401(k) plan, you have saved $2,700 over the year; therefore you have "earned" $1,224—the difference between $2,700 and $1,476—without doing anything other than not receiving the money. Do the math. Divide $1,224 by $1,458. What is the "rate of return"? Nearly 84%!

So, the first thing you do now is to join the 401(k) plan. Today. Put down the book, call your HR department, get the forms, and sign up. Why would you refuse that much free money from your employer and the government? Do it. Now. For the first year you will have to make investment decisions: where to hold the funds going into the 401(k) account each pay period. Frankly, pick and choose as you wish. At your age, the returns are nominal, relative to the 84%! It really doesn't matter what your choices are. The point of the exercise is to begin an investment program. You may choose to study what the funds are, how they invest, where, who the manager is. Great! The more you know, the better you will be able to make informed decisions. Ask others. Read the prospectus—always. Look online.

The objective will be to earn a 7% rate of return over the next 35 years—the 7% solution. If you do so, and if you never change jobs or increase your earning power with more education, or experience, or a new career—if you never do more than this initial step—saving 6% of your income each year, you will have accumulated more than half a million dollars: $562,702 to be exact. This would give you $3,282 monthly income during retirement!

The Second Lesson: The Power of Compounding. Again, you'll have to decide where to invest within the 401(k) plan. These plans offer a fairly wide variety of investment and savings choices. The choices are typically mutual funds, or some variation on that theme. Start easy. Assuming this is appropriate for your age and risk tolerance, consider putting 25% into the money market account, or the fixed account, if it is offered. Consider putting 25% into a corporate bond fund. You may have a choice such as Pimco, Fidelity, Vanguard, or the like. Choose one. Divide the other 50% between two or three equity funds, one being an international or global fund.

As you learn from experience, from others, and from learning, you will become more involved in deciding where and how much to allocate your savings. If you follow the ideas expressed here, you will develop a stop-loss strategy, an awareness of where to look for income producing securities, and an ability to change your mind when the facts change.

Don't forget to have the withholding amount on your paycheck changed. By deferring some of your wages, you should also reduce the amount sent away for taxes. Use the W-4 form from your HR office. It is a fairly simple IRS form that helps you determine how much in taxes should be withheld from your gross wages. For example, in the above example you may find that you can change your withholding from 1 to 2. You do this to immediately reap the reward of the taxes not paid—the $324. If you are paid biweekly, the result is not much—$12.46 a pay period. But you should keep that $12.46, rather than send it away to the tax authorities, only to have to claim a refund next April.

The Third Lesson: Investing for the Long Term. Once you have gotten used to saving over the next year, once you have received a few statements from the 401(k) plan administrator, once you have seen your savings grow, you may be ready for the next step. Each year increase the amount you save. You might save half of your salary increase. You might increase your savings by 1% of salary a year. You might decide on a fixed amount you want to put aside. But to increase your return, increase your savings into the plan each year. You are paying yourself first, before anyone else, including the tax authorities. It is the best game in town!

The Fourth Lesson: Patience and Persistence. Saving a portion of your earnings each payday for 35 years is the most powerful investment idea you will learn. You become the first bill each month: the first payment you make will go from the payroll department to your savings/investment account. It will rise and fall in value. You will open your statement envelope with joy or in fear. As you grow with your account, new ideas will present themselves. Try them out. This is your personal laboratory. Experiment to the extent that the investment choices within the plan allow.

It is not a lottery. It is not a casino. Do that with other money, with funny money, money you can afford to lose. The experiments you may do here are smaller, more controlled. As an idea, you may wish to try investing overseas. Learn the difference between international and global investing. Read the prospectuses on each of the funds. Learn what, where, how, and why they invest. Put the fund ticker on your computer, in your cell phone: Yahoo! or Google it to look inside. Think of it as a car you want to test drive. Watch the stocks it holds. Read about them. Relate them to your lifestyle—what product do you use that they produce? What service do you employ in your daily life?

Form opinions slowly, very slowly. None of us know which investments will do well, which will be meager, which will be dogs. No one in my profession has any idea. Financial professionals have opinions: some more educated, some more clearly expressed, some more succinct. These are opinions, not facts. We are more artists than scientists. Take all you learn, all you hear, with a grain of salt. Skepticism is your strongest suit in this card game. So, as you gather information, as you learn, be prepared to change your mind when the time comes. Few investment ideas stand the test of time. Many refuse to die a timely death, certainly.

Those who patiently and persistently save for retirement will increase their financial power many-fold. Readers of this book who have already saved face a retirement considerably more comfortable, more independent, and more worry free than those who have neglected the process.

Advanced Tax Planning Ideas: The Power of Giving

There are many advantages to making gifts to charities. The first and most important is the gift itself. You are helping someone in need, supporting a cause in which you believe, tithing because it is what you do. Every other reason for making a gift pales in comparison. If you have been a lifelong supporter of your church or synagogue or charity, read on. The tax and income benefits can be quite generous.

Charitable gifts can offer indirect income advantages, because the gift you make each year is tax deductible. Your tax bracket determines the amount of the tax deduction you may take for the gift. It can vary between 0% and 50%+. The deduction can be viewed as an income source. If you get a 33% tax deduction between federal and state, the cost of your contribution will be reduced by one-third. You can also view this as an increase in your income, as you do not pay the 33% in taxes you would owe if you made no contribution. This is the simplest way to view income from charitable contributions.

More complex views include charitable trusts. These can be either lead trusts or remainder trusts. A lead trust enables you to gift an annual income stream to a charity from a set amount of capital over a period of time, usually more than ten years. At the end of that time, the asset belongs to whom you wish: your heirs or a charity. If a charity, you get another tax deduction for the gift. If your heirs, the asset has passed to them outside of your estate.

A charitable remainder unitrust (CRUT) offers income and a tax deduction in response to your support for the community—the registered nonprofit of your choice. You define the community as you prefer. Your charitable intention is paramount here. These decisions usually follow a lifetime of contribution to your community. Your church or synagogue, a health institute, a non-profit, a non-governmental organization (NGO): any of these can be the recipient of your largesse. If you wish, you can name a number of organizations and filter the gift to many.

In exchange for making a deferred capital gift to a charity—in the form of a charitable remainder trust—you receive income for your life or lives, a current income tax deduction, and the profound sense of having made a substantial contribution. The amount you give is also a gift. It is removed from your estate. The heirs do not receive it. You must be fine with this!

The tax deduction is a function of your age, the amount of the gift, the interest rate for the trust, and the federal mid-month rate (FMR). Most often, an appreciated asset such as real estate is placed into the charitable trust. It is sold by the trust and no taxes are due upon the realized gain. The cash is placed into an income generating portfolio and it pays out at least 5% of the value of the trust each year to the grantor (you). If the trust grows in value each year, you receive 5% of a greater amount.

Let's use an example to illustrate. Assume a couple, ages 61 and 64, has a duplex that has appreciated over the past 20 years. It has been nearly fully depreciated. They net 3% income after all expenses and they are, quite frankly, tired of being landlords. They have been active in their church for their entire lives, having met in daily vacation Bible school. Their financial advisor suggests that they consider a CRUT. The duplex deed would be granted to the trust. They name themselves as trustees. The trust has a 6% distribution rate. When they pass away, the trust assets will revert to their church mission.

Value of Gift	$500,000.00
Age of grantors	61 and 64
Payout rate	6%
Frequency	quarterly
FMR	3.5%
First year's income	$30,000.00
Tax deduction	$122,320.00

The tax deduction's annual use is limited to 50% of their adjusted gross income. What amount they do not use the first year can be carried forward for five more years until it is consumed. At their combined tax bracket of 35%, it is worth $44,912 to them. That is, it reduces their taxes by that amount. This happens to be 9% of the current value of the property, a decent return from the Feds!

The resulting income of $30,000 in the first year and tax elimination of $44,912 more than triples their current income. The first four and a half years of income from the CRUT is, effectively, free income because of the write-off. Once the tax deduction is used up, their income has still doubled from the rental. Each year hereafter, their income will be 6% of the value of the corpus in the trust. If it grows by 2% each year, so does their income. They are free of the concerns of property management. They have made a significant gift to the missions in the future. They will have to file a tax return each year for the trust. The asset, no longer in their estate, is passed over by their children. Should they wish, they can change or add beneficiaries to the trust as long as each beneficiary is a tax-qualified non-profit as defined by the IRS.

An alternative to the CRUT is the gift annuity. A gift annuity is sponsored by a charity to which you make the gift of cash or appreciated property. A recently illustrated example comes from the Jewish National Fund (www.jnf.org):

Age	Rate	Tax Deduction per $10,000
65	6.0%	$3,110
70	6.5%	$3,594
75	7.1%	$4,155
80	8.0%	$4,695
85	9.5%	$5,099
90+	11.3%	$5,615

Your gift earns income distributed to you at the rates listed, given your age at the date of the gift. This income continues during your life. The Jewish National Fund receives the corpus of the gift at your death. You also receive the significant tax deduction shown above.

Taxes are a burden, one shared by most who work, who employ, who place capital at risk. Laws—and their bedfellows, regulations—are the imposition of that burden by those in charge. A burden lightly placed can be borne well. Burdens are not necessarily evil. They can result in infrastructure that benefits an entire community. The excessive imposition of burdens—particularly upon those who work, who employ, and who endure risk—reduces the quality of life for all participants: workers, employers, risk takers.

Albert Einstein reportedly once said that taxes were "too difficult for a mathematician. It takes a philosopher." No matter what your philosophy, understanding the tax system will empower you to reduce your tax burden and increase the power of your portfolio.

WORKSHEET

Assignment: Investigate and discuss tax opportunities prior to year end.

1. Visit the following website. Have fun with this one! IRS.gov

2. Speak with your financial advisor, estate attorney, CPA, and charitable representative about lead trusts and CRUTs.

3. Meet with your CPA in August to discuss the year's tax progress and to begin formulating tax ideas for the upcoming year.

14

GETTING THE
MOST FROM YOUR
RETIREMENT YEARS

"We will either find a way, or make one."
—Hannibal, on crossing the Alps in 218 BC

R etirement is that time in life when we can work or play as we choose. We become the custodians of our future. We work for ourselves, rather than a boss. We design our life around the things that matter most: family, community, travel, society.

In closing, let's examine a few scenarios from real life. These folks are actual clients, each enjoying their own particular world of retirement. These people have several things in common. They applied the lessons of their parents well, all of their lives. They faced retirement with fear and excitement, but with level heads, too. They had general guidelines, but no specific expectations for their futures. And for all of them, retirement remains an adventure that they wholeheartedly embrace.

◆◆◆

Jan and Michaela were successful professionals. He had a consulting business and she had a pediatric practice. At the time they retired, they had accumulated $1.8 million, had a monthly mortgage payment of $3,500 for six more years, and would be eligible to draw from Social Security in eight and nine years, respectively. They had two daughters and four grandchildren in two distant states. Today they enjoy working in their community and participating in church activities, including going on mission each year. Their current income need is for $8,100 monthly, or a 5.4% distribution from their portfolios. While both are quite intelligent, they have little interest or time for the work of portfolio management. They are quite comfortable now, in their twelfth year of retirement. An increase in income a few years ago has taken further pressure off the portfolio and allowed for even more travels abroad.

◆◆◆

Dennis worked as a mechanic all his life. His dad owned a garage in New Jersey. His savings were made easier because he had no children. As Dennis entered retirement, his dad passed away suddenly, leaving him with a valuable property 3,000 miles away. After a few years of EPA issues and regulatory work, he was able to sell his dad's garage business and keep a few hundred thousand. He lives modestly in the home he owns freely in the Ojai Valley of California. His career has become his hobby—a twist on the IRS assumptions. He buys a wreck, strips it down, pulls the engine and rebuilds it, then sells the "new" old car on eBay or locally. It is more a labor of passion than of gain. His garage is cleaner than many kitchens I have visited! His $400,000 is at work earning him the 6% he requires to supplement Social Security income.

He is also a master of Tai Chi and instructs those of us who are beginners in the ancient art of defense. The simple joys of life have also stirred him to write a volume of poetry. In short, he is quite the Renaissance Man.

•••

Despite having known Carol and Ben for more than 25 years, I still haven't a clue what Ben does for a living. I suspect it is that way for a reason. His strength is extraordinary for a man in his late sixties; his connections within the government are quiet, never discussed. She is the very successful owner of a placement agency, having retired from the Department of Defense 22 years ago. The business is an important part of her life, one she is loath to give up. They supplement their business income with returns from their portfolio, looking for a 4.25% distribution yield from $850,000, or $3,000 monthly. I have discussed the sale of Carol's firm with them for the past 15 years and have actually gotten close twice. Each time, a technical issue prevents the close. That is probably for the best. As I discuss with all business owners, you should expect to earn far more from your business than from your assets. Given the risks of ownership in today's highly regulated and taxed society—particularly for those most successful—you should expect at least a 30% return on your invested capital. Even if you sell it for five times that amount, the net proceeds after taxes would barely provide you with half of the pre-sale price. The ultimate challenge of success may be illiquidity.

•••

Rose has been a retired teacher for nearly 30 years. She has an excellent state retirement pension from the teacher's union. A widow, she married a second time in the early 1980s. Her second husband ultimately came down with Alzheimer's. She cared for him for nine years. Her son was also taken by Lou Gehrig's disease in a very short two years. She has been remarkably active in her community and has established a charitable remainder unitrust. Her pension, the CRUT, and a comfortable $2 million portfolio allow her to enjoy an active tennis-and-travel social life in her early eighties. The distribution requirement for Rose is 5.6%.

+++

As you can see from these examples, capital is saved to support a comfortable lifestyle during retirement. The lifestyle determines the distribution rate. The markets are of secondary importance. Mr. Market brings information daily. We choose to buy or sell as need dictates. His calm demeanor or frivolous antics are at best an interesting distraction from the otherwise fulsome days of retirement. He provides information and occasional entertainment, nothing more.

You will embark upon this voyage of retirement and it will take you through the rest of your life. Every departure for a trip has concerns. You prepare. You dream. You save. Then the day arrives and you depart. There is a certain excitement in the air as you face the unknown.

View retirement as a gateway to a new and different life. You have worked and saved for this all of your career. Now is the time to start fresh. While some trepidation ensues, that's okay. The challenge of the new will bring forth your natural skills.

You have been a saver and a tither. You use debt moderately and spend modestly. These habits will continue to stand you well. The economics of your future will depend upon the economics of both your family and of the nation, in that order. You will be surprised at how busy you become as your journey progresses, at how your costs stay within your means, and at how important your health has become.

> **View retirement as a gateway to a new and different life.**

Anticipate a long and successful journey. You should look forward to three or four more decades of a healthy life, an enjoyable lifestyle. It will eventually decline in complexity, becoming simpler. You will find richness expressed in that newfound simplicity. This journey ahead will be fractious and challenging, joyful and sorrowful, painful and pleasant.

The riches of the future are less about monetary units than about the richness of life; about the joy you and your spouse find, about the wise stewardship of your resources. The monetary units are your currency, they are not the voyage. As in the parable of the three servants who were given funds by the master to protect, you are the servant who was wise. Retirement is the story of what happens after the parable ends.

Enjoy your journey.

Eat wisely.

Sleep well.

Love with abandon!

WORKSHEET

Assignment: Review your health portfolio:

- With your spouse
- With your physician

There you have it. A few dictates from the masters. A few pathways through the Underverse of the Web.

Keep what you kill. You have earned the dividends and interest. Now take long walks, ignore the media, and learn a new language!

ENDNOTES

Chapter 1

1. Wendell Milliman, *Society of Actuaries Journal*, April 2009
2. *Statistical Abstract of the United States*, US Census Bureau, 2007
3. United Nations Demographic Commission
4. *The Next Hundred Million* by Joel Kotkin (New York: Penguin, 2010), pp.184-185.
5. Joel Kotkin, Ibid.
6. *Statistical Abstract of the United States*, US Census Bureau, 2000
7. *Wall Street Journal*, 11/14/09
8. J. Dew, Utah State University, 2009: Couples with financial assets vs. excessive debt are more likely to have happier, long lasting marriages: *Wall Street Journal*, 12/12/09.
9. Ruth Helman, Craig Copeland, and Jack Vanderhei, "The 2010 Retirement Confidence Survey": *EBRI Issue Brief*, No. 340, March 2010.
10. In a mature economy, export driven sales tend below import sales. Aware consumers shop globally. Less mature economies draw capital in, creating surpluses. These two realms functioning normally tend to force down advanced economy currencies while driving up "emerging" economy currencies. Thus, the US dollar has slowly depreciated over the past thirty years. This natural economic course has aided US income investors by giving impetus to their non-USD holdings—added value to the income stream.
11. Boston College Center for Wealth and Philanthropy, John Havens and Paul Schervish, 2006; *New York Times* 3/26/06: "Inherit the Wind."

12. RAND Corporation, Michael Hurd and James Smith, 2006. *New York Times*, op. cit.

Chapter 2

1. Start with Benjamin Graham's *The Intelligent Investor*, 4th edition, 1962, with commentary by several who followed his approach.
2. "In 44 years of Wall Street experience and study, I have never seen dependable calculations made about common stock values, or related investment policies that went beyond simple arithmetic or the most elementary algebra. Whenever calculus is brought in, or higher algebra, you could take it as a warning sign that the operator was trying to substitute theory for experience, and usually also to give to speculation the deceptive guise of investment." *The Intelligent Investor*, p. 570, 6th edition; 1962 Collins Business.
3. *The Intelligent Investor* by Benjamin Graham (New York: Harper Business, 1949.)

Chapter 5

1. Jeremy Siegel, *Stocks for the Long Run* (New York: McGraw-Hill, 2012).
2. Ned Davis Research, November 2009.
3. *The Strategic Dividend Investor* by Daniel Peris, (New York: McGraw-Hill, 2011), pp. 17-29.
4. A 9/6/10 *Barron's* article cited Douglas Cliggot of Credit Suisse, Barry Knapp of Barclay's Capital, David Kostin of GS, Bob Doll of Blackrock, Jeff Knight of Putnam, Henry McVey of MSDW, and Michael Ryan of UBS.
5. A simple definition of free cash flow: income minus expenses.
6. Total return = dividend + capital gain.

7. Stakeholder = owner, shareholder, employee, community, supplier.

8. A fashionable discussion during the High Middle Ages was, "How many angels can dance on the head of a pin?"

9. They also represent more than 40% of the total return for the S&P 500 Index, 1990-2010.

10. Cashing in a portion of a portfolio each year to meet income need with capital gains accretion.

11. There are more than 17,000 publicly traded companies in the US, including mutual funds, ETFs, UITs, et al.

12. Three hundred twenty-six foreign stocks pay some dividend, as well, and are listed in the US.

13. The payout ratio is another key indicator that attempts to describe the firm's ability to balance the need to keep cash on hand with the desire to distribute dividends. It can also be used as a filter, often successfully. The result is a shorter list, but a viable one, of 11 stocks with yields between 6% and 11%.

14. Style is defined as either size (large cap = $5 billion+ in capitalization, midcap = $1 to $5 billion, small cap = $250 million to $1 billion and microcap is less than $250 million) or strength (growth, value, or blend).

15. Occasionally, if a cumulative preferred stops paying its dividend, the owners may get voting rights in the interim until dividends recover.

Chapter 6

1. Firms like this usually destroy themselves and many participants.

2. In some cases, the top of the junk pyramid can be useful (BB-B) when the economy is functioning in a normal fashion. The yields at the top of this market can be an effective driver to the

portfolio design for 7%. Like BDCs and MLPs, used with discretion and knowledge, these can increase the portfolio's yield. As much as 5% to 10% of a portfolio may be placed in BB-B bonds with short duration and 6%+ yields.

3. Try *A History of Interest Rates* by Sidney Homer and Richard Sylla (Piscataway, NJ: Rutgers University Press, 1991).

4. Salomon Brothers, "What a Difference a Decade Makes."

5. Attributed to Baron Rothschild during the Communard uprising in Paris, 1874. As the city was in riot, with barricades evident from the windows of the Bourse in the City of Lights, floor brokers begged the Baron for guidance. We may still profit from his words.

Chapter 7

1. Investing in mutual funds involves risk, including possible loss of principal. Investors should consider the investment objectives, risks, charges, and expenses of the investment company carefully before investing. The prospectus contains this and other important information about the investment company. You can obtain a prospectus from your financial representative. Read carefully before investing.

2. An investment in Exchange Traded Funds (ETF), structured as a mutual fund or unit investment trust, involves the risk of losing money and should be considered as part of an overall program, not a complete investment program.

3. However, an investment in ETFs involves additional risks such as not diversified, price volatility, competitive industry pressure, international political and economic developments, possible trading halts, and index tracking errors.

Chapter 8

1. US Census, 2010.

2. Fixed annuities are long-term investment vehicles designed for retirement purposes. Gains from tax-deferred investments are taxable as ordinary income upon withdrawal. Guarantees are based on the claims paying ability of the issuing company. Withdrawals made prior to 59-1/2 are subject to a 10% IRS penalty tax and surrender charges may apply.

3. Variable annuities are long-term, tax-deferred investment vehicles designed for retirement purposes and contain both an investment and insurance component. They are sold by prospectus only and guarantees are based on the claims paying ability of the issuing company. Withdrawals made prior to 59-1/2 are subject to 10% IRS penalty tax and surrender charges may apply. Gains from tax deferred investments are taxable as ordinary income upon withdrawal. The investment returns and principal value of the available subaccount portfolios will fluctuate so that the value of an investor's units, when redeemed, may be worth more or less than their original value.

4. The Rule of 72 is a mathematical concept and does not guarantee investment results nor function as a predictor of how an investment will perform. It is an approximation of the impact of a targeted rate of return. Investments are subject to fluctuating returns and there is no assurance that any investment will double in value.

Chapter 9

1. As per prospectus, June 2011.

2. Investors should consider the investment objectives, risks, charges and expenses of the investment company. These considerations are outlined in the prospectus, and it should be

read before investing. A prospectus can be obtained from your investment professional or by contacting the BDC directly. There is no guarantee that the BDC will achieve its investment objectives. Investing in private equity and private debt is subject to significant risks and may not be suitable for all investors. These risks may include limited operating history, uncertain distributions, inconsistent valuation of the portfolio, changing interest rates, leveraging of assets, reliance on the investment advisor, potential conflicts of interest, payment of substantial fees to the investment advisor and the dealer manager, potential illiquidity, and liquidation at more or less than the original amount invested.

Chapter 13

1. *Gregory v. Helvering*, Court of Appeals, 2nd Circuit, 1934.
2. You may also have another trust account: an irrevocable trust springing from the death of your spouse, a charitable trust resulting from a substantial gift to the community, or even a corporate account held in the name of your successful business. Each of these has specific tax treatments for dividends, interest, and capital gain. Learn these before you invest.
3. For the background and methodology behind IRA issues, Ed Slott has written well on the subject. View his website and buy his book(s). It will be well invested capital.

REFERENCES AND RESOURCES

WEBSITES

Retirement:	SSA.gov
	Charitynavigator.org
Bonds:	investinginbonds.com
	Emma.msrb.org
	Bondsonline.com
BDCs:	bdcs.valueforum.com
	Quantumonline.com
MLPs:	naptp.com
	Hellenicshippingnews.com
	Quantumonline.com
	Ipaa.org
	Dividenddetective.com
Preferreds:	quantumonline.com
	Preferredstockinesting.com
	Preferreds.com
CEFs:	quantumonline.com
	Dividenddetective.com
	Sec.gov
	Cefa.com
Div stocks:	dividendinvestor.com
	Thediv-net.com
	Dividenddetective.com

Stock analysis: FINVIZ.com
Wikinvest.com
Nasdaq.com/asp/guruanalysis
Stockscreen123.com
Seekingalpha.com
Freestockcharts.com
Tickerspy.com
Vectorvest.com
Finra.org
Nyse.com

Economy: businesscycle.com

BOOKS

These are separated into four sections, leading off with the author's "must have" list, then books on markets, society, and economics.

MUST HAVES FOR YOUR BOOKSHELVES

The Intelligent Investor by Benjamin Graham, 4th edition, 1973, Collins Business
Certainly the most important book you will read on the subject, particularly this edition.

Stocks for the Long Run by Dr. Jeremy Siegel, 2012, McGraw Hill
The new edition, just out, is freshly updated and second only to *The Intelligent Investor*.

The Black Swan by Nassim Taleb, 2007, Random House
This book is third in importance after *The Intelligent Investor* and *Stocks for the Long Run*. Taleb's understanding of risk and its outliers—which are actually quite normal—are key to your designing your own portfolio.

A Random Walk Down Wall Street by Burton Malkiel, 1973, 2011, Norton Press
The fourth book for your library. The new edition is rewritten to your advantage. Take it down and enjoy the pleasure of fine writing.

Beating the Business Cycle by Lakshman Achuthan and Anirvan Banerji, 2004, Currency Books

By the founders of the ECRI, one of the very few organizations able to accurately predict broader economic cycles. Follow their Friday commentary on the website for an overview.

How to Read A Financial Report by John Tracy, 2004, Wiley
Along with Graham's "The Interpretation of Financial Statements" from 1937, the best approach you will find for guiding you to a better understanding of how to read company financials. If you want to dig deeper and broaden your numeracy skills, this is the template. Easy to read and apply.

A World of Wealth by Thomas Donlan, 2008, FT Press
If timing is everything, the May 2008 release of this important gem tells the tale. Read Donlan for the sheer joy of reading. An apologist in good stead for Adam Smith against the dystopian minions of Keynesian madness, the author also happens to be excellent at wordcraft. Enjoy.

Markets

Securities Analysis by Benjamin Graham and David Dodd, 6th edition, 2009, McGraw Hill
For the stalwart reader. Dated, yet comprehensive in its approach at the feet of the master.

Bonds by Hildy Richelson, 2007, Bloomberg
The definitive guide to the how and what of fixed income investing. Tells the story from inside, but with insight for the individual investor. Read this if you enjoyed investinginbonds.com. Venture forth only after doing both.

Preferred Stock Investing by Doug K. Le Du, 3rd edition, Book-locker.com, Inc., 2009
An excellent guide to preferred investing; website subscription and updates included.

The Ultimate Dividend Playbook by Josh Peters, 2008, Morningstar
Writer for the publisher's monthly newsletter; well stated dividend yield workings.

Inside the Yield Book by Sidney Homer and Martin Leibowitz, 1972, Bloomberg Press
The basis for virtually all bond analysis, perhaps to be read after *The Intelligent Investor* and before *Securities Analysis*. Significant, yet readable. You will need to take notes here.

Free Cash Flow and Shareholder Yield by William Priest and Lindsay McClelland, 2007, Wiley.
A brief, readable, and thoroughly enjoyable approach to the financial concept of free cash flow. Important.

Income Investing Today by Richard Lehman, 2007, Wiley
Safety and high income through diversification is the subtitle. This is an excellent, fairly academic approach to all the themes discussed herein. A book for every retiree as a primary reference tool.

Dividends Still Don't Lie by Kelley Wright, 2010, Wiley
The newest version of the Geraldine Weiss classic from which we all learned. Ms. Wiess and Mr. Wright remain among the premier sources of stock investing information and guidance.

The Dividend Investor by Harvey Knowles, 1992, Irwin
Dated certainly, but still a good introduction to analyzing stocks for income and safety. The principles don't change, simply the members on the lists.

The Strategic Dividend Investor by Daniel Peris, 2011, McGraw Hill
How to find dividend stocks from a CFA who does it for a living.

Retire Secure! by James Lange, 2009, Wiley
A CPA and attorney, Lange does a good job of covering the technical bases with chapter reviews, cartoons, and plenty of charts.

Are You a Stock or a Bond? by Moshe Milevsky, 2009, FT Press
Professor from the IFID Centre in Canada; good detailed exposition on real retirement costs, inflation, and—most importantly—longevity risk.

Fooled by Randomness by Nassim Taleb, 1999, Random House
Earlier work, somewhat more mathematical, still useful as a follow up to Black Swan.

A Demon of Our Own Design by Richard Bookstaber, 2007, Wiley
The book on the history of hedge funds, the risks they manage, the ones they create, and their inherent instability—or how to make millions while losing billions.

Tom Dorsey's Trading Tips by Tom Dorsey, 2001, Bloomberg
The master of technical analysis (from whence most of the current work originated). An excellent way to discover stock trends analysis. A system that works more often than most.

The Four Pillars of Investing and *The Intelligent Asset Allocator* by William Bernstein, 2002, McGraw Hill
Each of these books is rigorous in its application of the efficient frontier, asset allocation, and MPT. While I disagree, I respect his strength. He willingly skewers Wall Street "thought leaders."

Your Complete Retirement Planning Road Map by Ed Slott, 2007 Ballantine Books
Ed is the expert on retirement plans—IRAs, 401(k)s, et. al.— as well as on beneficiary issues. How the estate handles these accounts is vital to your estate planning and Ed is the lead author on the subject. He is well respected as both an author and speaker.

The Investor's Manifesto by William Bernstein, 2010, Wiley
The final voice of the master; short, to the point, acerbic. Read with glee and with caution. Dictates abound from a wizard who offers no quarter.

Irrational Exuberance by Robert Shiller, 2000, Princeton Press
The prescient text on markets and their manipulation. Dr. Shiller remains well regarded for his timely remarks today. One of the first to refute the mathematical astrology of financial mechanics.

The Future for Investors by Dr. Jeremy Siegel, 2005, Crown Business
The good doctor's prescription for investors remains in line with Mr. Graham's. Bernstein, Biggs, and Shiller all agree that investing for the long run means the shareholder, vs. the share flipper, wins.

The Single Best Investment by Lowell Miller, 2005, self published
A good guide to Mr. Miller's takes on dividends and their value to your portfolio.

The Big Investment Lie by Michael Edesses, 2007, Berrett-Koehler
Wonder why your advisor has the yacht and you have the dinghy? This book pulls no punches. It should have been far more successful—I wonder why it wasn't?

Don't Count on It! by John Bogle, 2011, Wiley
Mr. Bogle inveigles against the industry and its thieves.

Benjamin Graham on Value Investing by Jane Lowe, Penguin Books
The biographer of Graham puts out a smart little book of quotes from the master: "Interesting possibilities abound on the financial scene, and the intelligent and enterprising investor should be able to find both enjoyment and profit in this three ring circus. Excitement is guaranteed."

Enough by John Bogle, 2009, Wiley
The title says it all: stop with the excessive bloodsucking of the mutual fund industry.

The (Mis)behavior of Markets by Benoit Mandelbrot, 2004, Basic Books
The publisher's name should be in the title. Probably the most scribbled-in book the author owns, it begs the obvious: markets are turbulent and unpredictable. Enjoy.

The Myth of the Rational Market by Justin Fox, 2009, Harper Collins
An easy read of the debacle we all enjoyed during 2008, told by a master story weaver.

Gone Fishin' Portfolio by Alexander Green, Agora, 2008
The lazy man's guide to investing, controlling costs, enjoying life.

The Wall Street Journal Complete Retirement Guidebook by Kelly Greene, 2007, Dow Jones
One in their series of how to invest; a good overview of investing, maximizing SSI, etc.

Are You a Stock or a Bond? by Moshe Milevsky, 2009, FT Press
Professor from the IFID Centre in Canada writes a good detailed exposition on real retirement costs, inflation, and—most importantly—longevity risk.

Mad Money by Susan Strange, 1998, U of Michigan Press
An intellectual's journey through money mismanagement at all levels, before 2008!

The Investment Answer by Daniel C. Goldie and Gordon S. Murray, 2011, Business Plus

SOCIETY

The Generosity Factor by Ken Blanchard & S. Truett Cathy, 2002, Zondervan
A restaurateur tells a fable, one we all know. Simple. Well worth the refreshing read.

The Wisdom of Crowds by James Soroweicki, 2004, Doubleday
If you get this story, you will enjoy your retirement, free from the troubling influence of noisemakers and trouble seekers. There is a certain group intelligence that is simple and profound. While the

majority are lemmings marching ever to the sea, collective wisdom (not collective society or media) can be powerful and truthful.

Where Good Ideas Come From by Steven Johnson, 2010, Riverhead Books
"Go for a walk, cultivate hunches, write it down, keep your desk messy, embrace serendipity, make mistakes, borrow ideas, and take on hobbies."

The Art of Contrary Thinking by Humphrey Neill, 1954 Caxton Press
"When everybody thinks alike, everyone is likely to be wrong." It should have been the subtitle here.

Why Success Always Starts with Failure by Tim Harford, 2011, Farrar, Straus & Giroux
An editor from the *Financial Times* gives a good viewpoint from Europe on conflict and adaptation.

It's Getting Better All the Time by Stephen Moore and Julian Simon, 2004, Cato Institute
One hundred trends in human and earth culture that cannot be denied. Simon was the winner of the wager with Paul Erlich (of population doom infamy). His ability to frame a question so as to best understand its implications, assumptions, and denials is famous. Open it at random every time you feel depressed!

The Improving State of the World by Indur Goklany, 2007, Cato Institute
We are living longer, healthier, more comfortable lives on a cleaner planet than ever in human history. Try that line at your next dinner party. It's sure to get a conversation started, but read this first.

A Splendid Exchange by William Bernstein, 2008, Atlantic Press
Another extraordinary piece by the master of financial history.
(All right, the author admits to the enjoyment of history.)

In Defense of Globalization by Jagdish Bhagwati, 2004, Oxford
Press
Like Goklany, a tremendous mind, to be enjoyed in his knowledge
and wordcraft. To deny the validity of globalization is to refuse a
comfortable retirement.

The Docks by Bill Sharpsteen, 2011 UC Press

The Box by Marc Levinson, 2006, Princeton
Both of these are devoted to you the steelworker, you the long-
shoreman, you the stevedore, you the midshipman, you the truck-
er, who have made this story possible. Enjoy the miracle of ideas
turned into wealth.

The World Is Curved by David Smick, Penguin, 2008
Getting past the economics drivel of Friedman's flat world to a
fairer image of global economics, the importance of globalization,
and the strange incestuous world of global finance.

Against The Gods by Peter Bernstein, 1996, Wiley
A history of the management of risk; a fascinating story of man's
search for financial wealth.

Capital Ideas by Peter Bernstein, 2005, Wiley
The history of Wall Street and its idea masters.

The Forgotten Man by Amity Shlaes, 2008, Harper
An historian of the first magnitude, Ms. Shlaes tells a gripping tale and takes an entirely new perspective on the history of the Great Depression.

Gross National Happiness by Arthur Brooks, 2008, Basic Books
Interesting social science read of humans' interaction with one another and the markets; a very positive view of the world of Man.

Wall Street Revalued by Andrew Smithers, 2009, Wiley
The dark side of Man, markets and obscene profits run amok.

ECONOMICS

The Black Swan by Nassim Taleb, 2007, Random House
This book is third in importance after *The Intelligent Investor* and *Stocks for the Long Run*. His understanding of risk and its outliers—which are actually quite normal—are key to your designing your own portfolio.

Beating the Business Cycle by Lakshman Achuthan, 2004, Currency Books
The founders of the ECRI, one of the very few able to accurately predict broader economic cycles. Follow their Friday commentary on the website for an overview.

Calculated Risks by Gerd Gigerenzer, 2008, Simon & Schuster
How to know when numbers deceive you.

The Power of Gold by Peter Bernstein, 2000, Wiley
An accurate history of the base metal's influence on mankind.

Worthless yellow metal has determined the outcome of wars and economies—and will continue to do so.

How to Read A Financial Report by John Tracy, 2004, Wiley
Along with Graham's "The Interpretation of Financial Statements" from 1937, the best approach you will find for guiding you to a better understanding of how to read company financials. If you want to dig deeper and broaden your numeracy skills, this is the template. Easy to read and apply.

A Mathematician Reads the Newspaper by John Allen Paulos, 1995, Basic Books
A brief introduction to how to understand numbers in print.

Innumeracy by J.A. Paulos, Hill & Wang, 1988
Helps the reader understand the math of investing simply and with fun.

The Mathematics of Investing by Michael Thomsett, 1989, Wiley
Excellent reference tool for the basics and intermediate analysis of investment math.

The Best Book on the Market by Eamonn Butler, 2008, Capstone (Wiley)
As Director of The Adam Smith Institute, Butler offers a clear understanding of how and why capitalism works to the benefit of society. A short, definitive read worthy of the three hours.

The Wealth of Nations by Adam Smith, 1776, various
The primer on how capitalism works. The 18th century prose can be a chore today, but simply reading the story of the pin maker is worth the effort.

The Secrets of Economic Indicators by Bernard Baumohl, 2005, Wharton

A reference book to review when the next statistic emerges from the maws of DC. The guide to how statistics are constructed and what they do and do not tell you.

Damn Lies and Statistics by Joel Best, 2001, University of California Press

How they fool you with numbers and how little they actually know about the math of investing. A must read for anyone who intuitively knows they are lying but doesn't quite understand how.

Useless Arithmetic by Orrin Pilkey & Linda Pilkey-Jarvis, 2007, Columbia Press

More a social treatise on how the social engineers want to rule, yet the basic guidelines are applicable to the investment process. Question, understand, learn.

Applied Economics by Thomas Sowell, 2004, Basic Books (also Basic Economics, 1998)

Once you read Sowell, you will find it difficult to deal with the social engineering of most other writers in economics or finance. He makes it both easy to understand and infuriating that these thoughts are so thoroughly ignored.

ARTICLES

Since Bengen's 1994 article, the history of the 4% Rule—the assumption that you should never take more than 4% from your portfolio—can become very tedious, very quickly. Nevertheless, for those interested in both original documents and their history, these articles can provide significant information. The most important new discussions are from Scott, Sharpe, and Watson in Journal of *Investment Management*, 3Q/09, and from Cooley, Hubbard, and Walz, *Journal of Financial Planning*, 4/11.

Milevsky, Moshe A. (2005). "Real Longevity Insurance with a Deductible: Introduction to Advanced-Life Delayed Annuities (ALDA)," *North American Actuarial Journal*, 9(4): 109–22.

Milevsky, Moshe A. and Wu Shao, Ling (2011). "Annuities and Their Derivatives: The Recent Canadian Experience," in O.S. Mitchell and J. Piggott, eds., *Revisiting Retirement Payouts:Market Developments and Policy Issues*. Oxford, UK: Oxford University Press.

The Bible, King James Version, Matthew 25:14-30. The parable of the master who distributes his talents to three servants holds timeless wisdom. Recommended reading!

ACKNOWLEDGMENTS

Martha Lawrence, as editor, has taken a rough stone lying in the field and shaped it into the diamond in your hands. In addition to her wordcraft, she has the ability to "cull the herd." More than half of the original manuscript lies upon the cutting room floor, to your good advantage, dear reader. Martha's heartfelt support remains invaluable.

Jared Kuritz of Strategies PR has engineered the process from first draft to published work. His efforts have taken the author from obscurity to wherever I stand today. Guidance, forbearance, and strong coaching skills are his true worth.

Gwyn Snider has applied her design skills to the task of this cover and interior. Her leadership has brought forth this effort to the light of day.

Letty Soliz has been my office manager for more than ten years. She has grown in her position and taught me how to better serve our clients. My thanks to her for unfettered devotion to them, to the wordcraft, and to me.

Sharon, my dear friend and wife, is the inspiration for this work. She saw what I could not: a vision of helping others, simply by reaching out. The book is a gift to each of you, from her, through me. Thank you.

ABOUT THE AUTHOR

John Graves, ChFC, CLU has spent 26 years advising people how to become better stewards of their resources. As an independent financial advisor, he focuses on designing and maintaining clients' portfolios consistent with their needs, rather than some market paradigm. John is a Chartered Life Underwriter and Chartered Financial Consultant through The American College in Bryn Mawr, Pennsylvania.

He has traveled extensively, with more than 80 countries' stamps in his passport. His avocation is adventure. He has sailed to Hawaii several times as well as across the Atlantic and throughout the Mediterranean and Caribbean. He has trekked the Andes, the Sahara, the Taklamakan, the Serengeti, and the Namib.

In his previous career, John was a chef. He does enjoy a fine meal with a nice Bordeaux or Montalcino.

John agrees with Benjamin Graham that the search for value is far more interesting than a brief joy ride in the markets. His passion is sharing his knowledge with others so that they, too, might embrace all that life has to offer. For more information, visit www.theretirementjournal.com or email John at jgraves@west.net.

GIVING BACK

When you give, you share your wealth and receive infinite goodness in return. One half of the proceeds of this book will be divided among these three charities:

Adaptive Sports Foundation: Since 1984, this organization has provided profound, life changing sports experiences for wounded warriors and people with physical and cognitive disabilities, as well as for those with chronic illnesses. For more information, visit www.adaptivesportsfoundation.org.

The Ojai Foundation: This organization fosters practices that awaken connection with self, others, and the natural world. This mission is fulfilled through the foundation's semi-wilderness, sustainable-model educational sanctuary in Ojai, California, as well as through its Council in Schools and Counsel Training initiatives. For more information, visit www.ojaifoundation.org.

Tostan: This organization empowers African communities to bring about sustainable development and positive social transformation based on respect for human rights. Since 1991, Tostan has brought its holistic 30-month education program to thousands of communities in ten African countries: Burkina Faso, Djibouti, The Gambia, Guinea, Guinea Bissau, Mali, Mauritania, Senegal, Somalia, and Sudan. For more information, visit www.tostan.org.

INDEX